SAVING AMERICA

In the face of national crisis, a congressman pleas for the nation to restore its trust in God

BY
D. EVERETT WATSON, II

www.deverettwatson.com

ISBN-13: 978-0692457429

Printed in the United States of America

TABLE OF CONTENTS

DEDICATION

To our grandchildren-Brianna, Kelly, Jordan, Lucas, Amy, Justin, and Alivia; that they will always stand for Christ.

ACKNOWLEDGMENTS

I wish to personally thank the following people for their contributions to my inspiration, personal understanding, and other help in creating this book:

My wife Brenda, for her unconditional devotion to our relationship, my ministry, and her support through this entire project.

My parents, Rev. Donald and Carol Watson, who taught me to love and fear God, and the importance of standing true to Jesus Christ.

Several personal friends or associates who aided me by providing their insight in U.S. foreign policy, political issues, legal and practical considerations; Rev. Lamar Hahn, Rev. Jeff Scurlock, Rev. Branden Barlow, Dawn O'Neill Stone, David Poli, and Joah Billingsley, my proof-reader.

And I thank each of you, my readers. I trust that this book will be a blessing to you, and inspire you to stand for truth among a society who has long forsaken this rare virtue.

Everything we do in life is a result of collaborating with individuals who have the wisdom to help fill in the gap between our personal expertise, and areas that we are not as well versed in. This eighteen month (plus) project was a massive undertaking, and I appreciate each of these, as well as several others not mentioned, who made your important contribution toward bringing it to its completion.

INTRODUCTION

Chris Edwards is a young freshman representative from South Carolina. He won his congressional seat nearly a year ago, and has already become disillusioned by all the economic, political and moral chaos he must face each day. Overwhelmed by national unrest and so much corruption in Washington, he began to ask himself, *"What would happen if America were to return to the Judeo-Christian values it was founded on?"*

In the company of so many older, established leaders, his thoughts of a national reform were stifled by the fact that he was too young and inexperienced as a congressman, to make an impact on the nation. He felt like a college fraternity pledge, who had to "pay his dues" before becoming a full-fledged member of the brotherhood to take a more active role in the political process. But he had been elected to serve, not sit. Now he is faced with a decision; represent his country by the moral principles that it was founded upon, or compromise and disappear into an invisible sea of politics. Little did he realize that his decision might save the nation, or lead to its final decline.

PREFACE

On Wednesday, September 14, 2004 several families gathered at our Church in south Alabama for shelter, waiting for Hurricane Ivan to make landfall. Our inland town gets the medium to strong tropical storms or occasional weaker hurricane winds as vestiges of the storms that periodically hit Pensacola or Mobile; but the experts were predicting a strong hit, and everyone listened and got prepared. About 10:30 PM, the lights went out as the wind grew stronger. Several neighbors lay under the pews in the sanctuary praying, with tears in their eyes, afraid of what would happen once the storm hit our town. Around 3 AM emotions escalated when we heard the forecaster on a battery operated TV announce that the eye of the storm was just 30 miles away and would be on us within minutes. I read some Scripture by the light of an oil lamp to comfort everyone who had gathered in the fellowship hall, and then prayed for God's protection through the storm. Strong, sustained winds battered the town, downing hundreds of pine trees and dozens of oaks. A large pecan tree hit the roof of the sanctuary, causing water to pour inside the building. The wind speeds at the airport just a few miles away were clocked at 125 mph. The next morning several of us went outside to survey the damage while wind gusts were still strong enough to blow a grown man down. There were downed power lines, trees and debris laying everywhere. The streets were impassable. Our Church building suffered over

$50,000.00 in damages, but we survived one of the worst storms ever to hit the State of Alabama.

Today, a storm of much greater magnitude is sweeping throughout America, threatening to destroy the entire nation; not a natural storm, but one that is shaking the spiritual, moral, economic and social foundations of our great land to the core. Some of those who sought shelter from the hurricane that I wrote of may have never set foot in a Church building since that night. And many people today are turning blind eyes to these grave threats to America.

In 1989 Charles Colson wrote, *"...a crisis of immense proportion is upon us. Not from the threat of nuclear holocaust or a stock market collapse, not from the greenhouse effect or trade deficits, not from East-West relations or ferment in the Middle East. Though all these represent serious problems, in the end they alone will not be our undoing. No, the crisis that threatens us, the force that could topple our monuments and destroy our very foundations, is within ourselves. The crisis is in the character of our culture, where the values that restrain inner vices and develop inner virtues are eroding. Unprincipled men and women, disdainful of their moral heritage and skeptical of Truth itself, are destroying our civilization by weakening the very pillars upon which it rests."* [1] How much more relevant are these words to us today than when they were written 25 years ago?

The idea for this book was birthed several years ago during a tremendous upheaval against our country's Judeo-Christian heritage. While written as a fictional novel, it addresses forces at work in our lives that are very real. As I was writing down my ideas, some of the hypothetical situations on my mind were actually beginning to take place around the nation. Others may have already occurred in time past, while we were merely becoming more aware of their happening with the increased hostility against our Christian values. By the time this book is published, these events may have become old news, and replaced with even more critical issues.

Modern Christendom has fallen prey to a dangerous philosophy that we must adopt a new gospel in order to be relevant to our culture. There is no such teaching in Scripture to back this up. Instead, the Church is called to be change agents, as "salt of the earth," [2]   In the midst of popular preaching that embraces a "more relevant message," we are warned by the apostle Paul not to accept any message not found within the pages of the Sacred Scriptures. [3]

Many Americans today claim Christianity as their religion, yet have never opened a Bible in their lives. Church has become synonymous with the average social or civic organization. The title, *Christian* is often used to authenticate us as being socially acceptable, or to gain political favor.   But when the name was first used in Antioch it was a title of contempt, because this group of people patterned themselves after the most radical teacher who had ever walked the earth; the son of a carpenter, who claimed to be the Son of God. This man named Jesus, preached against every sin, but also proclaimed a message of love, hope, and forgiveness of sins.

Today, while we openly embrace the anti-Christian values that threaten the moral foundations of this nation, we have diluted these Scriptural teachings in order to remain in the favor of those around us.   If the Lord does not return soon, we will once again face ridicule and persecution if we choose to pattern our lives after the Christ of the Bible. Indeed, this is already beginning to happen in America. In the last two years alone, there has been an increasingly growing wave of hostility toward Christianity while, overseas, Christians are being slaughtered for their faith by the hundreds. We as a nation look on with indifference as the enemies of Christ taunt our beliefs, threatening to dominate our own land.

There is nothing gray about this novel. It is not intended to merely entertain, but to inspire you to take back the true meaning of Christian living in America. Although we live in a period of tremendous national decline, it's not too late for our nation. America is falling apart, but we can see her restored to her former glory. There have been notable moments of our history when America was straying from its spiritual foundations; but when men and women repented and surrendered in obedience to God's Word, she experienced revivals within the churches that spilled over into every aspect of secular society. These times of widespread spiritual renewal were brought about when men stood and fearlessly proclaimed the pure message of the Bible; men such as George Whitfield, that fiery evangelist from England whose preaching in the mid 1700s played a major role in the First Great Awakening in the American colonies; the ministry of Congregationalist minister Jonathon Edwards in Northhampton, Massachusetts, whose preaching also played a vital part in this spiritual awakening;   and John Wesley, the father of modern Methodism.

A pastor recently told me that "Revival, as we once knew it in American churches is a thing of the past. It will never happen again." Sadly, this philosophy has been accepted by thousands of ministers across the land. But the Bible teaches us that this is not so. [4]   The writer of the 85th Psalm cried out to God, *"Will you not revive us again, that your people may rejoice in you?"* [5]   If another great revival of Christian conscience and living were to sweep this land, it would certainly have different characteristics than all of the other historical times of spiritual renewal-but it would reap the same results: Churches would begin to fill, people would repent and change their ways of living, the marketplaces would change and honesty would once again be the norm for everyday living. The economy would be healed, and our politicians would operate on a totally different plane, because Christians would put good moral men and women in office.

The American political system has proven that it cannot solve the complex problems of our society. Neither Democrats nor Republicans can secure our welfare or security. The more I study the Bible I am more convinced that the key to solving all of these problems is stored within its pages. I contend that Jesus Christ is our hope, and outside of Him, there is no hope. This book is intended to provoke you, the reader to see what could occur in our society, or what could be changed for the better if God's people repent and fully return to Him. When God's power is unleashed, nothing can hold it back.

Remember the age old statement, "United we stand; divided we fall?" One of the things that made our nation strong was the unity of a common stand for truth and freedom, even though there were lesser issues that everyone might not necessarily agree on. But over the past several years, an indifference to many of these principles have moved us beyond the unity we once took for granted, driving deep wedges between families and friends, associates and even within the Christian Church. These concerns that have polarized Christians could become issues that unite the Church if it experienced a God-sent revival that returns us to our knees and back to the pure message of the Bible. If the Church will unite in Christian love, the nation will follow.

It is imperative that we be aware of the ever-increasing dangers that threaten our freedoms. We must be sensitive to others that do not hold to our Judeo-Christian beliefs, but at the same time take a stand against policies that threaten to quench the Christian presence from every element of our society. Dr. Robert Jeffress, Senior Pastor of First Baptist Church, in Dallas Texas said, *"...we do the world no favors when we [Christians] refuse to talk about what God has declared to be truth."* [6] And world renowned evangelist, Billy Graham also said, *"Our society strives to avoid any possibility of offending anyone-except God. Yet the farther we get from God, the more the world spirals out of control."* [7]

If this book should rouse your emotions, my prayer is that it will provoke you to your knees in passionate prayer for a national revival. If we ever needed to cry out to God for America's salvation, the time is now.

1

A Nation in Peril

The audience erupted with cheers at the Civic Center auditorium in Greenville, South Carolina. Delegates to the Constitution Party National Convention stood up in thunderous applause as Senator Randall Smith walked across the stage holding his wife, Martha's, hand, and surrounded by his three children. He waved to the members of the convention in appreciation for their support. After a long fought battle between Temple Hollingsworth, the only remaining candidate in the Constitution Party's primaries, the Convention nominated him as the party's candidate for President in the November elections. Earlier in the year three other presidential hopefuls had withdrawn from the race, shortening the drawn out primary process.

As the applause dwindled, Senator Smith and his family left the stage and exited the auditorium where their car was waiting. Thousands of audience members began filing out onto the parking lot to a mild April evening. A stir of excitement lingered in the air as Constitution supporters embraced their party's nominee. All were hopeful that his election would start a turn-around in the country's direction in just a few short months.

Scott Crawford accelerated down the ramp leading to Interstate 85. The pastor, from the small town of Blue Ridge Heights, South Carolina was taking a quick run to Charlotte, North Carolina to drop his teen children off at his father's house for a visit during spring break. His wife, Connie sat next to him reading while Jordan and Brianna were settled comfortably in the back seat. Sixteen year old Jordan was absorbed in the game he was playing on his I-pad. Their daughter, fifteen year old Brianna took in the scenery as they traveled down the road. 40 year old Scott adjusted his seat and settled back for the remaining drive to the town where he grew up. His mind raced while thinking about everything that he needed to accomplish. He had planned to spend more time with his aging father, but a death in the Church disrupted his weekly routine; he needed to get back in time to finish his notes for Sunday's message. Time flew by quickly, and Scott turned onto the exit ramp to leave the interstate. A few minutes later, he turned off the road onto a long dirt driveway leading to his father's house. He could see his seventy-five year old father, walking across the yard toward the barn. Bill Crawford looked up when he spotted the car approaching the house. The elderly man turned back to the driveway to greet his family as they got out of the car.

"Grandpa!" Brianna exclaimed, grabbing her grandfather. Bill took his granddaughter in his arms with a tight squeeze, and reached out to give Jordan a hug as he approached him. He was delighted to see his family, and turned around to greet Scott and Connie when they got out of the car. "So good to see you, son; and you, Connie!" he greeted his children with a hearty hug. "Come on in and have a seat," he invited them inside. *"Everything still looks the same,"* Scott thought to himself as he looked around the house he grew up in. His mother had died two years ago. Her pictures and personal belongings still remained throughout the house. Things would never be the same without her being there, but these things were a cherished reminder.

The family spent the rest of the afternoon sitting in the family room, talking. It was refreshing for Scott to be home and spend time with his father. Although it was necessary to return to South Carolina the next day, he would have more time when they picked the children up next week.

Friday morning traffic in Washington D.C. was bumper to bumper as thousands of government workers rushed to get to work. Congressman Chris Edwards pulled into the parking garage of the Rayburn House Office Building at the U.S. Capitol and walked toward the entrance door. After a series of security breaches, the office complex adjacent to the Capitol Building had been placed under tighter security measures. Although it posed some inconvenience, he was thankful for the added precautions just the same. Edwards, a tall, slender man in his late thirties, had won a tight election, replacing his incumbent, a conservative congressional seat in South Carolina nearly a year ago.

The Constitution Party had morphed over the last decade from a traditional moderate-conservative party to a more defined group that stood for clear conservative principles. Members of the new Constitution Party were considered "right-winged radicals," although there were a few members who remained satisfied to carry on their "careers" as moderates. The House of Representatives was controlled by the Constitution Party, while the Progressive Party held the Senate. For the most, this party swayed to the far left; this resulted in gridlock which prevented the passing of numerous bills that were crucial to the country's stability. The continual squabbling among the legislators had numbed Edwards to the point that he had considered not running for a second term in office; but he wasn't ready to give in, yet.

As he headed toward his office, the young legislator tried to brush aside a recent thought that he couldn't shake from his mind; *"Given our national state of chaos, what would happen if America returned to the values it was founded on?"* The young congressman brushed the thought aside. He was in a hurry to take care of several pressing items, but seeing an older congressman, Representative John Campbell, a Constitution conservative from Louisiana approaching him down the corridor, he paused for a moment to talk.

From the outside looking to the Capitol Building, tourists who passed by wondered about what went on inside the impressive building of neoclassical architecture. Surrounded by so many monuments and historical buildings, they thought about the leading figures from the past; George Washington, Abraham Lincoln, Thomas Jefferson and dozens more whose statues stood throughout the city. These were the commanding men who had fought to build a strong and united nation. But from the inside, the elected leaders were occupied with a totally different world.

America was overwhelmed by numerous crises, politically, economically, and internationally. Violence rocked the nation from large cities and small towns alike. Just this year alone, there had been three major school shootings, senseless rioting that broke out in another major city threatening to destroy the entire town, and a hostage crisis had occurred in a large Church in Dallas, Texas. High ranking officials in the Justice Department turned a blind eye to even gross violations of the law. Nearly every branch of the federal government had been rocked by some type of scandal over the past three years. Most recently a whistle-blower had revealed that the IRS was targeting local

Churches, threatening them with loss of tax–exemption if their pastors voiced their personal political views, even in their personal lives. One Church discovered an undercover agent who was attending their worship services, trying to collect information that could incriminate them. CE-1

Pressure was building up around the nation; citizens were at the tipping point of not being able to tolerate any further corruption within the government. These overwhelming issues plagued Congressman Edwards' mind as he continued on to his office. It seemed as if no one was running the country. And no one seemed to care. He opened the morning paper to scan through the latest news before getting to his work. "SUPREME COURT TO HEAR CASE ON RELIGIOUS FREEDOM," the headlines read.

The city council of San Esteban, California had outlawed the public display of any symbols of faith eighteen months ago. This action was taken after a prominent citizen who was an atheist, had threatened to file a lawsuit against the city. He claimed that his rights were being violated when forced to see religious symbols such as crosses and even nativity scenes located on Church and private properties. Consequently, a number of churches in the City of San Esteban had been fined, and several pastors, priests, and a Jewish Rabbi were threatened with arrest for refusing to comply with the new law. This ordinance was upheld in the lower courts and had made its way to the U.S. Supreme Court.

An increasing climate of hostility toward Christianity was sweeping the country. Similar actions had begun to affect even smaller communities. Every day, it seemed, another anti-Christian organization was challenging a different area of the nation's Christian heritage. CE-2

And the nation was strongly divided over a host of other social issues; issues that would have been unimaginable several decades earlier. Forty five states had already legalized same-sex marriage. Several others had pending lawsuits before the courts to open the door to legally recognize the un-biblical relationships. CE-3 Edwards' own state was one of the few that had not yet given in to the demands of gay activists. *"But it is only a matter of time..."* the congressman thought to himself. The Christian Church was increasingly divided over the subject, with several major denominations now even ordaining homosexuals into the ministry. Activists were pushing strongly to stifle any opposition to the LGBT community. Some hoped to make it illegal to openly criticize anyone based on their gender identity. This issue was making the abortion debate seem miniscule, in light of all the conflict that surrounded it.

Edwards had been raised in a Christian home. Although he considered himself a good moral man, he had allowed his political endeavors to pull him away from all Church involvement. At times the congressman felt as if he was trapped in a raging inferno that no one could put out. The nation continued to weaken in its influence on other nations who had once looked to her for strength and leadership. *"America today is not the nation I was born in,"* Edwards thought to himself, as he sat down at his desk. "How could the United States continue to claim, *In God We Trust* as its national creed?"

As he laid the paper down, Edwards asked himself, *"How can I make a difference in the lives of those I represent?"* His strong desire to do that was quenched by the fact that he was too young and inexperienced to sponsor any meaningful legislation. After all, he was a freshman congressman. The unwritten rule expected the newer politicians to "pay their dues" before introducing any legislation of their own. Yet, Edwards was not one to sit still. He had come to Washington to represent his fellow citizens, and was resolved to do his job with integrity, even if it meant going against the establishment. Now he was faced with a decision; represent his state and country according to good moral principles, or compromise and disappear into an invisible sea of politics.

The lawmaker opened his laptop and plugged it in the wall. Congress would be on leave for the next two weeks, and he couldn't spare the luxury of trying to save the nation today. He struggled to get this thought out of his mind so he could focus on a mountain of work that had to be done before he left for the weekend. This was the first time he and his family had gone home since moving to Washington. While much of this time would be spent in setting up a new State office in Columbia, he looked forward to spending some time with family and friends as well.

Jessica James, Congressman Edwards' executive assistant knocked on the open door and entered his office. The young woman received her Bachelor's Degree only a year ago, and joined the congressman's staff not long after he was elected to office. She aspired to enter the world of politics herself, and was delighted for the opportunity to work as a congressman's assistant so early in her career. An experienced staff would have made the transition into his new public life go much smoother; but the previous assistant had retired. Nevertheless, Edwards' decision left him with a good feeling, knowing that he had given a newcomer an opportunity to get her foot in the door. After all, it wasn't that long ago that he had struggled for his own chance to enter the professional world. "Here is the agenda for today's session," she said, laying a folder on the congressman's desk before returning to her desk in the adjoining office.

Chief Justice Norman Henderson sat behind the ornate desk in his chambers, reviewing the case summary of *The Church vs. San Esteban, CA*. Having traveled through the lower courts, the Supreme Court had elected to review this case based on the merits of its threat to religious freedom. The case was of such nature that all nine of the justices had unanimously agreed to hear arguments. This was a notable action, since the approval of only four justices were required to bring it to the high court.

A legal assistant knocked on his door, indicating that oral arguments would begin in five minutes. Henderson picked up the summary and left his chambers. He stepped out into a long corridor where the associate justices were gathered. When all nine were assembled, they walked in unison to the doors standing behind the massive bench where each of them sat in the nationally recognized courtroom. Justice Henderson walked through an opening between two other entrances, followed by Bob Harmon and Susan Semmes, the two senior associate justices. The lower associates entered through the doors on either side of the center. Each of the nine justices ceremoniously took their seats together. Justice Henderson looked out over the courtroom that was filled to capacity with lawyers, legal assistants, aides to congressmen, and a few lucky citizens who were close enough in line to secure a seat in the packed venue. The Court Marshal instructed the audience to be seated, signaling the start of the morning arguments. "We have reviewed the legal briefs of both parties in the case entitled, *The Church vs. San Esteban, California*," Justice Henderson opened the session, his voice echoing through the spacious courtroom. "At this time we will entertain the position of the Church."

24

Jeff Godwin, the attorney for the San Esteban Association of Christian Churches, approached the podium situated in front of the nine justices. The attorney was from Greenville, SC, known as "the buckle" of the Bible-belt because of their strong adherence to biblical values. He was retained by the Church association because of his experience in arguing similar cases. In fact, Godwin had appeared before the Supreme Court three times previous to this case being heard today.

"Mr. Chief Justice," the middle-aged lawyer respectfully addressed Justice Henderson, "I will argue the merits of our case based on its violation of the First Amendment to the U.S. Constitution." He opened his argument slowly and clearly. The attorney's voice echoed through the court room in a confident, yet commanding tone. Mr. Godwin articulated his argument in a logical sequence, not going into many details of the previous trials, but instead focusing on several key points that reflected on how the religious rights of the Churches he represented had been violated. Each of the nine justices listened to his oration carefully, which he brought to a close in less than twenty minutes, notably shorter than his allotted time. For the next several minutes the justices asked him pointed questions to clarify the specifics of his case. Five of the justices held conservative views, although two of these had sided with the more liberal four in several previous cases. While the experienced attorney normally could get a feel for juries and judges while representing clients in lower courts, he had no sense of direction on which way the nine justices would rule in this case.

The sound of hurried footsteps echoed through the Rotunda of the Capitol building as Congressman Edwards made his way across to the House Chamber on the south wing. The spacious room was flanked by 23 relief portraits of great leaders from around the world who had made some significant contribution to the development of law through the centuries. A marble relief of Moses hung prominently on the north wall where the Speaker of the House was ceremonially seated. As Edwards approached his desk, his eyes met the face of this great Bible character. For a moment it seemed as if the thundering prophet who wrote the very Law of God was watching his every move. *"If Moses were living today, would he throw down the tablets of the Law in anger over the national sins of the people, just as he did over three thousand years ago?"* Edwards wondered. [8]

After the morning session began, the day passed by swiftly for Edwards. Although the congressman was devoted to his work, today his mind was far from the business that was taking place. Again, the thought crossed his mind; *"What would happen if our nation returned to the moral values it was founded on; just what if the people would reject this new philosophy that America was no longer a Christian nation?"* He couldn't understand why this question kept coming to his mind. Perhaps it was his conscience ringing back all the Bible lessons from Sunday school while growing up. Or maybe, just maybe it was because he was in the middle of the most powerful ruling body in the world and had been called to take a stand when no one else would?

The call for adjournment came just as quickly as he entered the House Chamber. Young Edwards tried to shake these thoughts from his mind as he stood to leave with the other representatives. All those around were unaware of his personal disconnection from the day's business.

Nancy Edwards, Congressman Edwards' wife, pulled into the parking lot of their condominium located in the Independence Towers on the edge of Arlington, Virginia. The drive for both

Edwards and his wife was only about five miles from the Capitol, but took a minimum of 20 minutes to commute each way. Having grown up in the town of Princeton, West Virginia, the medium height, slender brunette in her late thirties was still having a difficult time adjusting to the bustle of large city life. She wasn't considered a socialite, like many other wives of prominent leaders, and only attended major events with her husband.

Nancy had secured an ideal job working as the executive volunteer coordination director for the national offices of Emergency Preparedness International. Her job, while demanding, was very rewarding, providing an outlet to be a positive influence on many people throughout the entire United States. Just in the last four years, five major hurricanes had hit the United States, and a major earthquake rocked the state of California, leaving thousands of families displaced from their homes. These events had raised awareness for the need of better equipped volunteers to respond in such disasters. Most state and local chapters had limited resources or volunteers, so when the national office received Nancy's resume and saw her qualifications she was immediately hired to re-organize the national volunteer training program. Regular interaction with the staff of local chapters kept her busy equipping them with the tools necessary to enlist a strong volunteer response team. As an employee of the national office she was also a first responder in the event of a national disaster. Having just returned from a training session in Arkansas, she spent the day catching up on a long list of administrative duties that had accumulated in her absence.

Nancy parked her car, got out and entered the condo. Exhausted from a long day at work, she laid her handbag on the table, and leaned back in a recliner in the living room for a few minutes. She felt a surge of refreshing energy as she relaxed, waiting for her husband to arrive.

The congressman's wife picked up the TV remote and turned the television on. The music for the United Broadcasting Corporation national evening news had just finished playing and the camera zoomed in on Marvin Maddox, the evening news anchor. "Good evening, and thank you for watching the UBC Evening News," he opened the broadcast. "Today, the United States Supreme Court heard arguments in the case of *The Church vs. City of San Esteban, California.* The plaintiffs contend that their first amendment rights were violated when the city council enacted an ordinance that bans all public displays of religious symbols. This ordinance includes Churches and private properties, where crosses and even nativity scenes can only be displayed on the inside of their buildings. A ruling is expected to be handed down in late May or early June."

"Now, going to the upcoming presidential elections, the first of a number of debates will take place between the Constitution Party candidate, Senator Randall Smith and Progressive Party's Senator Roger Francis. The first debate will take place on the second Monday night in May. The main focus of this debate will be economic and foreign policy issues."

Nancy's mind wandered from the television to what she would be doing later on that afternoon. Their 16 year old twin sons, Justin and Jamie, were spending this week at spring football camp. Tonight Chris and Nancy were attending a banquet to honor freshman congressmen and their families. While she had been waiting for this week's visit home, Nancy also looked forward to meeting some more wives of the newcomers to Washington, and perhaps establishing a new friendship. She stood back up to greet her husband when she heard his footsteps, and kissed him affectionately as he walked through the front door.

After changing into formal attire for the evening social, they drove to the George Washington Grand Hotel and went to the main ballroom where dozens of congressmen and their wives were already assembling. Chris scanned the large hall and walked toward a table near the center of the room when he spotted an older senator and his wife. William Hudson, from Charleston, South Carolina was in his second term and already raising eyebrows around the nation with his outspoken persona. "Good evening, congressman," the senator stood to greet Edwards as they found a seat directly across from him and his wife, Rebecca. The two legislators immediately struck up a conversation, and their wives began to talk among themselves.

"So, what's the latest from the House?" Hudson asked Chris after they were settled in their chairs. "We were hoping to work on the immigration bill, but the conflict in the Middle East has been taking most of our time," Congressman Edwards replied. "Yes, it's becoming more unstable," Hudson agreed. "The latest intel reports are indicating some unrest between Israel and the Palestinians." He paused to take a drink of his coffee. "The President has indicated his intentions to put pressure on Israel to back down." Congressman Edwards leaned toward the table. "I can't support such a move," he interjected. "If *we* were attacked by another country, it would be war all over again." Senator Hudson nodded thoughtfully. "You're right," he agreed. The night progressed, and the two congressmen continued to talk about other pressing issues. Edwards sensed genuineness in the senator. Their relationship had been forged when they met while Chris was campaigning for office. The congressman felt that tonight it had been cemented.

Scott and Connie Crawford rolled back into town after a short but refreshing visit at his father's home. The drive was only two hours away, but the pastor was unable to get home as often as he liked. "At least we're as close as we are," he thought to himself. His first pastorate was in Bluefield, West Virginia, near Princeton, where he met Connie, and married. For fifteen years he had been over 200 miles away from home, but after moving to Blue Ridge Heights, he was thankful to live within reasonable driving distance from his aging father. The Crawford family had been called to the Trinity Church almost a year ago. The young pastor was still in the "honeymoon" stage of his new pastorate, getting to know his Church members more personally, as well as the extended Church family who returned to visit on occasion.

A pickup truck approached their car on the country road as they neared their house. Lucas Hall, its driver blew his horn and waved to the couple as he passed. Lucas had grown up in the Trinity Christian Fellowship, and was a faithful member until several years earlier, when he lost his mother, and went through a difficult divorce-all within a 6 month period of time. *"That was the time he needed his Church family the most,"* Scott mused as they passed the younger man. Lucas also had a daughter, Emily, who was a schoolmate of Jordan and Brianna. He had custody of Emily, and faithfully devoted his life to providing a stable environment for her to live in. Although his ex-wife, Michelle was an alcoholic, and somehow didn't find as much time to spend with Emily as she could, the teenager knew she was loved by her father. She seldom expressed her feelings about her mother to him. As Scott thought about these circumstances, he breathed a prayer for Lucas, asking for the Lord to restore the joy for living that he once had.

Congressman Edwards and Nancy drove to the Reagan International Airport and began the familiar routine of a time-consuming security check before boarding their plane for North Carolina. They would land in Charlotte and drive the remainder of the way to Blue Ridge Heights. The flight was uneventful. Even as quiet as it was, the time seemed to pass by quickly as Chris reflected on the question that just wouldn't escape his mind. Nancy sensed his unrest but tried not to interrupt his thoughts, although they spoke occasionally. She assumed that he was concerned with a difficult issue from work and just couldn't lay it down. After landing at the Charlotte Douglas International Airport and renting a small car, they began the drive to his hometown. Blue Ridge Heights, situated in the foothills of the Blue Ridge Mountains was a charming town of only 6,000 residents with a rich heritage tracing back to early settlements of the Cherokee Indians. The congressman began to unwind as they slowly transitioned into their vacation mode. Nancy could see a physical change in her husband as he became more relaxed the closer they got to his old home. The couple continued to drive through the quiet, older community and entered the driveway of Chris' boyhood home.

Edwards was hoping to surprise his mother, but she had heard on the news that Congress was in recess and halfway expected a visit from her son. Judy Edwards was a short, gray-haired woman in her mid seventies, but was still very energetic and found it difficult to sit idle with everything she still had to accomplish. Her husband had passed away ten years ago, but her strong disposition helped her to come through her loss.

"I've been expecting you. Come in!" she exclaimed in delight when she saw them. "I'm so happy to have you back home!" Judy looked over their shoulders toward their car. "Oh, where are the boys? They couldn't come?" she asked hopefully.

"They stayed behind for spring football camp," Chris responded, giving his mother a tight hug. "They're growing all up," the elderly lady said, shaking her head. "But you tell them I'll see them the first thing after school gets out. No excuses!" She hugged Nancy and then turned to lead them into the kitchen, where the aroma of a country home-cooked meal drifted throughout the entire house. Judy and Nancy sat down and began talking while Chris carried their bags up to his old bedroom. After he finished unpacking the car, he joined them around the table.

"We were just talking about our new pastor," his mother told him as he sat down. "Tell me about him," Chris replied. He had been waiting to hear more about the new minister who succeeded his former pastor of many years. "Well, he is relatively young, perhaps in his mid-thirties," she responded. "He is married, and has two teens, a boy and a girl." She went on to say that although the Church had been disappointed when their longtime pastor of 20 years retired, the younger pastor and his wife quickly won their hearts as they demonstrated a genuine love and no partiality for each of the Church members. "Why don't you come to Church with me tomorrow?" she asked them. Judy had given her new pastor a heads up that she was expecting her son and family for a visit. She could hardly wait to introduce the pastor to her son, who was truly the pride of her life.

The young congressman felt a surge of warmth from her question and immediately told her that they would join her, much to his own, and Nancy's surprise. He was feeling the need for a Spiritual presence in his life, even though he hadn't shared this with his wife. Maybe it was from the return to his old hometown, calling him back to his roots? The Edwards spent the rest of the afternoon getting caught up on what had been going on in the small town with family and friends since they moved to Washington.

     The next morning Chris and Nancy accompanied their mother to the Trinity Christian Fellowship, slipping in the back door just as the minister of music began leading the congregation in an opening chorus. The Church was an older white-sided building with traditional architecture that seated 150 people, although it averaged around 45 members during the morning worship service. Even though it was over a hundred years old, it had been renovated just before the former pastor retired, and had a beautiful royal blue carpet and new padding on the pews. Chris and Nancy felt welcomed, and were warmly greeted with several smiles of the few who saw them come through the back door. Pastor Scott Crawford stood in front of a short padded bench on the stage. He greeted them with a warm smile when he saw them coming in. Chris recognized several of the older members, and noticed one or two families he had never met. Several teenagers sat on the back row across the aisle. He also noticed Wesley and Karen Crenshaw sitting several rows back. Karen was a history teacher, and Wesley had become a technology magnate in the south, having built a successful information systems company from a mere handful of employees to a present staff of over 3,000. As they joined the congregation in singing, both he and Nancy sensed a spirit of peace that neither had felt in a long time.

     Pastor Crawford's eyes connected with each of the members and visitors as he stepped behind the pulpit. He recognized the congressman and his wife since they were accompanied by Judy, who had spoken of them on several of his visits to her home. The pastor didn't call attention to them out of sensitivity to their prominent place of leadership, and simply gave a warm welcome to all visitors before he opened his Bible to read the Scripture text for his morning message.

"When I shut up the heavens so that there is no rain, or command locusts to devour the land or send a plague among my people, if My people, who are called by My name, will humble themselves and pray and seek My face and turn from their wicked ways, then I will hear from heaven, and I will forgive their sin and will heal their land." [9] Edwards was moved by the message, and could hardly wait to meet the pastor after the morning service was over. It seemed to the young congressman as if the pastor was preaching specifically to him; like he knew what had been going through the lawmaker's mind.

At the conclusion of the morning worship service, Chris and Nancy joined the other Church members in the aisle, greeting old friends, and being introduced to a few others they had not yet met. Judy slipped up to the pastor and invited him and his wife, Connie home for dinner. Today would be a double blessing, since he now had the opportunity to talk with the congressman personally at the Crawford's home.

Chris and Nancy sat down at the table with Scott and Connie and their mother, and held hands as the young pastor asked a blessing over the meal. Chris knew the pastor's time was precious, especially on Sundays, but after dessert he asked him if he had a few minutes. The two walked outside and sat down at a picnic table under the shade of a large oak tree in the back yard. As the two men talked Edwards began to open up to the pastor. "I started out believing that I would move to D.C. and actually be different than the establishment," he confided, "but just in one year alone, the environment has started to change me." Scott could see that the congressman was going through an intense personal battle. "In what way?" he asked. "Well, the mindset in

34

Washington is the total opposite of the morals I was raised to live by. It seems as if half either don't care what's going on, and the other half is possessed by money and power." He continued. "I can't begin to tell you the level of corruption that I face every day. The public would be horrified if they only knew some of the things going on behind closed doors."

The congressman struggled, trying to vent his emotions and hold them in at the same time. Scott felt his anxiety. He knew the congressman had a good heart, but felt as if he was at some kind of a crossroad. Chris Edwards didn't seem to fit the political mold, in his opinion. Now that he had gotten some of his frustration on the table, Edwards was ready to share his recent experience with the pastor. "As I was going to work last week, a question hit me almost as hard as a hammer," he explained. "This question has been going over and over through my mind, *'What would happen if our nation returned to the Christian moral values it was founded on?'* Not an audible voice, but just a strong impression." As he listened, Scott was convinced that Congressman Edwards would not be another average politician. "That question is going through the minds of many Americans today," he responded. "But you are in a place to address it." The congressman was reflecting thoughtfully on his response. "Have you considered that this might be a special call?" Scott asked him. "I'm really not sure what to think," the Congressman replied. "I'm just wondering how, even if it's possible, I can make a difference by myself."

The pastor's mind was racing. Just yesterday, he could never have imagined that in a few hours he would be sitting with a U.S. Representative and giving him advice. "You're facing an important decision." Scott spoke up. "Remember Moses from the Old Testament? When God called him, he was overwhelmed by his commission. After all, he had been told to challenge the king. He even tried to excuse himself from his responsibility, but God equipped him for the job." Edwards' mind flashed to the image of Moses in the House Chamber, whose eyes seemed to penetrate his soul each time he saw it. "And the prophet, Elijah," the pastor continued. "Even after he called Israel back to God, he still felt alone. But God reminded him that there were others still standing.[10] Even though you may not know who your allies are, stay close to God," he exhorted the congressman. "Let Him guide you, just as he did Elijah and Moses."

Congressman Edwards had an important decision to make in the upcoming days; a decision that could change his own life, and the future of the entire country. "Leadership is doing the right thing, only after much prayer, regardless of the consequences," Scott told him. Those words struck the congressman just as powerfully as the constant voice asking him that nagging question all along. He *was* at a crossroad; and he made his choice.

2

A New Outlook

Wesley Crenshaw looked up from his desk. "Come in," he spoke loud enough to be heard on the other side of the closed door. Jase Childers, the marketing manager for Web Connect, Inc. entered the room. The marketing executive handed Wesley a thick folder as he sat down. "This is my proposal for the new television ad," the executive introduced its contents to his boss. The large corporation already did business throughout the United States and even Europe. The technology giant had recently announced plans to open a new office complex in the heart of Atlanta, Georgia, and planned to establish another office on the west coast within two years. They had been working on the release of a new "Intele-phone" that would rival all other similar devices on the market.

The company's president thumbed through the first several pages until he spotted a spreadsheet. He appreciated the effort that his executive staff put into their work, but Wesley was a numbers man and always wanted to see the bottom line before taking on any new project. "Six million dollars," he read out loud and stopped, reflecting. Jase looked on with anticipation.

He knew that his superior expected quality, but that always came with a price. "How much time will this give us?" he asked his marketing manager. "Two months," he was ready for this question. "That provides coverage for the top 10 major cities throughout the United States." Wesley seemed pleased. "Not bad," he said. The two men discussed the upcoming campaign for the remainder of the morning.

After breakfast, Congressman Edwards prepared to leave for Columbia, the Capitol of South Carolina. Nancy stayed behind to spend some more time with Judy. As Chris drove through the town, he noticed the old office where he had conducted his law practice before going to Washington. His mind was flooded with memories from the past. While in his private practice, Edwards' dream was to one day go to Congress. This way he could impact more lives than his limited influence allowed in the small town. The lawmaker picked up speed as he left the town limits. He was scheduled to meet with Brad Lewis, his executive assistant for the new State office. Brad had studied Political Science, and the young congressman felt that his education, combined with his youthful zeal was just the right person to become his home office manager. He had already worked for several years as an assistant to the previous congressman. His experience, alongside the many relationships with other congressional staff members, made him the ideal candidate for the job. They had agreed to meet at the Cozy Corner, an old country café in a small community just outside of town, where hopefully they wouldn't be interrupted by any news media. The congressman entered the café and scanned the dining area for his new assistant. He spotted him a moment later sitting in a booth near the back and walked over to greet him.

Earlier that morning, Karen Crenshaw signed the teacher's roster at Blue Ridge Heights Academy before going to her classroom. She and Wesley were well liked by everyone who knew them, and took a genuine interest in those they worked with as well. The two were financially comfortable, with a stable teacher's salary and her husband's income as a corporate CEO.

The middle-aged teacher nodded to several co-workers as she hurried to her class. She entered the room and sat down behind her desk to review her week's lessons during her planning hour. Her eyes fell on the first page that read, *Comparing World Religions.* She was dreading this lesson because she knew that its content might seem controversial to some of her students. Not that she minded discussing the subject of religion, but she recalled a recent major outburst in a larger school district stemming from a mere discussion of the Ten Commandments between a teacher and her students. Karen was not one to rock the boat when it came to her work. *"I'll just skip that part of the lesson,"* she reasoned. *"After all most of our students are Christian-or at least have some sort of Christian influence in their lives."* She didn't realize that by trying to avoid conflict, she would soon be in the center of the largest controversy ever to come to the Appalachian School District.

Back in Columbia, Congressman Edwards prepared to wrap up his meeting with Brad. "Is there anything else about your previous experience that might be of benefit?" Edwards asked him as he began to wrap the meeting up. "It helps to have an extra pair of ears," Brad responded. "Word travels through the grapevine. If I ever pick up on anything of interest, I'll keep you posted." This was one more confirmation to Chris that he had made a good choice with Brad. A network of good relationships was vital to keeping in touch with the concerns of the citizens he represented. The congressman looked at his watch. It was nearly 2:00 PM. They had been at the café for three hours. The two men agreed to meet again before Edwards returned to Washington, and then left the café.

The National Progressive Party Headquarters bustled with activity. A strategy session for Senator Roger Francis' presidential campaign was underway with all executive staff members present. Thomas Wainwright, the senator's campaign publicist sat at the conference table waiting for Francis to arrive. The two were to meet before the entire campaign team held their first full meeting. Wainwright was a stocky graying man in his mid-fifties. His impeccable dress gave the impression more of a senator than campaign publicist. A few minutes later Senator Francis arrived and sat down across from his manager. As usual the senator was rushed, and cut right to the subject. "Here's a copy of my schedule so you can give me some prospective dates for the upcoming debates," he informed him.

The publicist paused to scan over the schedule. I see you're pretty tight for August, but we have a good head start. We can work that out with the Constitution Party's campaign team." He opened his planner and pulled out a pen. "Until then, I'd like to go over one or two pointers that are crucial to your success." He circled two items on his agenda. "First of all, and most importantly, avoid any controversial issue no matter how strongly you feel about it." The senator nodded. "The press can take anything you say and spin it out of control." Wainwright paused to be sure the Senator was following him. "Next, if you encounter any potential problem, call me immediately." He stood and walked out of the room. The publicist was known for his brevity. Francis felt fortunate to have secured the well-known strategist as his publicist. He came at a high rate, but the

Senator knew that his experience could save his campaign time and money in the long run.

Rev. Russell Taylor walked across the living room and sat down to read *The Princeton Times,* the daily newspaper. His usual routine of a morning cup of coffee over the newspaper had been disrupted today by a checkup at the doctor's office. After his appointment, the retired pastor and his wife, Ruby spent the afternoon with their daughter, and were just getting back home. He had barely sat down when the telephone rang. Taylor glanced at the caller ID and then picked up the receiver. "Hello," he answered. "Good afternoon, Brother Taylor," the voice on the other end of the line greeted him. "This is Scott Crawford." At first the older minister didn't remember him. "Scott who?" he asked. "This is Scott Crawford-you remember, from God's country, South Carolina," the younger pastor said jokingly. "Oh yes, Scott!" Now he remembered. "Well, you know what they say about West Virginia; it's almost heaven. We need to get together a bit!" He returned the humor. Rev. Taylor had always been active in his work as a pastor. Even after retiring, he found himself rushing to the hospital when he learned that a former Church member was sick. His heart was still in it, although his physical body was telling him to slow down. Six months ago, he had undergone a shoulder replacement and was facing another one after he had fully recovered from the first procedure. He sometimes felt that he was no longer needed, and wondered if he still had a place of service in the Church.

"So tell me," the older minister said to his younger counterpart. Is your Church growing spiritually?" Scott was struck by Taylor's question. Many of his former college classmates and other associates were more interested in how many Church members each other had or how large their Church

41

sanctuary was during occasional class reunions. But his mentor didn't seem concerned about what others around him considered as a success. "Well, sometimes I feel that we are, and there are other times that leave me wondering if I've even been doing my job," Scott responded to his question. "But some things have been happening just in the past week alone that I've never before encountered in my ministry." "Tell me about it." The older minister was interested. So Scott began to share his encounter with the congressman, and then the recent situation involving their children's school assignment.

"You know," the retired minister replied, "sometimes I think we spend months at a time wondering if we're making a difference in the lives of those that we serve." He sensed that the younger minister was struggling with these feelings, too. "But true ministry travels beyond the four walls of your own Church." Russell was preaching to himself. "Stand for the truth in this school issue. You will be touching more lives in the process." As they continued to talk, he realized that his own ministry wasn't over. He might not be playing an active role as a pastor, but he could offer his prayers and support for Scott and his ministry, and for greater influence through his new relationship with the congressman.

3

Conflict in the Classroom

The tardy bell rang at Blue Ridge Heights Academy, bringing a crowd of students through the classroom doors. Mrs. Crenshaw hurried from the cafeteria where she had duty supervising the students during her lunch break. Her students poured into the class as soon as she unlocked the door. After the bell rang, the middle-aged teacher called the roll and then passed out some worksheets entitled, *Comparing World Religions.* "Read chapter six," she instructed her students, "and then complete your worksheets. We'll discuss the answers when you have completed the assignment." The students began reading their assignments quietly.

Fifteen year old Emily Hall looked at the first item on the worksheet and took a closer look. Jordan Crawford raised his hand from the back of the classroom. "Yes," Mrs. Crenshaw acknowledged her student's hand. "Um, I'm just wondering why this is a chapter about comparing religions, but only one religion is discussed?" he asked. "There's only one reference to Christianity on the worksheet, and Judaism isn't even mentioned." Mrs. Crenshaw was taken off-guard by the question.

She had assumed that her students would do their work with no questions asked. The teacher decided to test her students' assumption. "This exercise just presents a different viewpoint on religion. Have you ever considered the possibility that they all could be right?" she posed. All students' eyes were on Jordan when they heard Mrs. Crenshaw's question. "What do you mean by that?" Jordan inquired. "The truth of the matter is," she asserted, hoping to quell Jordan's sudden participation, "these are the three major world religions, because they all worship the same God."

"I don't believe that, Mrs. Crenshaw," he challenged his teacher's assertion. "Christianity and Judaism do worship the same God, although most Jews don't accept Jesus as God's Son." The teacher was about to change the subject, but Jordan continued. "And the god of Islam is nowhere in the Bible." Jordan didn't mince words. His classmates snickered. "Whatever the case, everyone is entitled to their opinion," she replied and quickly added, "Go ahead and complete your assignment. We'll discuss it in class tomorrow." The class remained quiet and completed the assigned worksheet.

Forty year old Lucas Hall turned into his driveway, exhausted from a long day's work. The single father worked as an engineer for the local electrical company and enjoyed his work. While it was the ideal job, it occasionally required him to be out of town. He was leaving in two more days to work on a project in the lower part of the State, and was trying to decide how he should provide for Emily's care while he was gone. The last time he had to be out of town, she stayed with her mother. After coming home, he discovered that she had been away from the house nearly the entire time. When Michelle returned she was so stoned she didn't even know that Emily was there. Lucas always tried to keep his daughter from any conflict between him and her mother, but this time she had crossed the line. He made it clear that there would be no further visits until Michelle had gotten free from her addiction.

He opened the door and walked into the house to the aroma of supper cooking in the kitchen. Emily was mature beyond her age, and tried her best to help out around the house. She sat at the table doing her homework while keeping her eye on the stove. "What are you working on?" he asked. Sometimes she got tired of his constant attention to her homework, but she knew that her father cared enough to be checking, especially after such a long day's work. "A study guide for my history test." Emily handed him the paper she was reviewing. Lucas took the paper in his hand. It was headed, *The Five Pillars of Islam.* He read the first item slowly, aloud: "*Shahadah*-Declaration of faith- 'There is no God but Allah, and Muhammad is His prophet.'"

2. Salat-Prayer five times a day
3. Zakat-Giving a percentage of one's income to the poor.
4. Sawm-Fasting and self control throughout the month of Ramadan.
5. Hajj-A pilgrimage to Mecca at least once in one's lifetime if they are able to do so. [11]

Lucas stopped reading. "Just a minute," he laid the paper on the table. "What is this?" he asked his daughter. "We've been studying the major world religions. Mrs. Crenshaw gave us this handout in class today." She had her father's attention. "Would you believe that Jordan actually asked why there was even no mention of the Ten Commandments [12] or any other reference to the Jewish faith?" Emily asked her father. "Good for him," he responded. "I may ask her the same question." Lucas could see that she wanted to tell him more. "She even told us that all three religions worship the same God," Emily continued. Her father looked up with a start. "What?" Emily's teacher had crossed the line of teaching religious belief, and *non-Christian*, at that. [CE-4]   Although Lucas hadn't attended Church for several years except on rare occasions, he was still spiritually sensitive.   It was beyond his imagination that this was happening in their small town.

"You're mature enough to know right from wrong," Lucas told his daughter. "Don't ever compromise your beliefs." He was suddenly smitten by a feeling he hadn't experienced in years. How could he expect Emily to do what was right when she saw the way he lived?   He knew that if he didn't soon become the example that he should be, she might lose any spiritual interest she still had. The young father tried to get the thought out of his mind.   *"Maybe I should share this with the pastor on my way out tomorrow morning?"* he thought to himself.

Connie Crawford glanced up from her desk when the reflection of a vehicle entering the Church parking lot flashed through the window. She stopped working on the spreadsheet on her computer and looked up to greet Lucas as he walked through the door. "Good morning!" she greeted him with a smile. "Good morning, Connie," he returned her greeting. "Is Scott available?" The pastor had already stepped out of his office when he heard someone speaking. "Come in, Lucas. It's so good to see you!" He noticed an uncomfortable expression on the other man's face. "Let's step in my office," he invited Lucas into his study. "What can I do for you today?" he asked, as they sat down. Scott normally spent a few minutes in casual conversation to help set his visitors at ease, but Lucas was probably on his way to work. Lucas felt guilty for coming to the pastor for counsel after he had all but forsaken his Church life. But he told the pastor about his daughter's class assignment. Scott understood the seriousness of what he was hearing; what made it so touchy was that the teacher who was involved was a member of their Church.

"You know," he said after a long pause. "For years we have been looking from inside a small fish-bowl to the world on the outside; all the time just thinking all these things that happen in larger cities doesn't affect us. But even in a small town, the devil is going to attack us any way he can get his foot in the door," he continued. "What better way than to challenge our children's Christian beliefs?" Lucas nodded in agreement. Scott leaned forward in his chair. "I'll discuss this with Steve; and why don't you talk with Kelly Graham about your concerns?" Steve Williams was the Academy Principal, and also the Youth Pastor at Trinity Christian Fellowship. Kelly was the new school PTA president. "The PTA can be a strong advocate for the parents; and I have no doubt that Steve will be in your court." Lucas had already thought about the PTA, but wasn't sure if this would be the best way to start since Karen was more than likely an active member too. Scott sensed his reluctance and said, "I'll be praying with you for a peaceful outcome." The pastor knew that the fathers' concerns, as valid as they were, could be blown into a full-scale conflict around the town. Lucas was comforted by the pastor's advice. It had been a long time before he had spoken with anyone in the Church. He left, longing to have the fellowship restored with these people he had known for so long.

After Lucas left his study, Scott couldn't help but think that his ministry might be at a turning point. Until now, he hadn't faced much controversy in his ministry. It was interesting that he had been sought out earlier by Congressman Edwards about his ideas that would more than likely cause a stir in Washington. And now, he sensed another conflict on the horizon; one that could affect his family, and the entire community. In spite of these apparent crises, it was a joy to bring healing to these needs. The pastor pulled out his keyboard tray and began composing a letter to the congressman.

Dear Chris,
It was a pleasure and my honor to have met with you recently and share your concerns for our country. Your courage has been an inspiration to me. Be assured that I will pray for you daily, for wisdom and courage to stand firm in the face of your challenges. I look forward to talking with you again soon.
Sincerely,
Scott

Two weeks passed quickly for Congressman Edwards as he and Brad worked diligently to complete setting up his satellite office in Columbia. Now, back in Washington the congressman could already feel the disharmony that seemed to flood the Capitol. He picked up his telephone and placed a call to Senator Randall Smith from Florida. Chris had spoken with him several times over the short time that he was in office, and believed that the senator might be open to his thoughts. The older senator was ordinarily quiet spoken; whenever he stood to speak on the Senate floor, he usually had something of value to say, and his colleagues respected his words. The senator had a prior appointment but assured Chris that he would call back when he was available. This would give him time to develop his thoughts more clearly. Smith could be his greatest ally for getting support from the Senate, or his worst nightmare. As he hung up, he began thinking of other congressmen who would either support, or oppose his efforts.

Since the resolution would start in the House of Representatives, the first person he thought of, of course, was the Speaker of the House, AJ Wilson. Wilson was a member of the Constitution Party from Arkansas. Although his views were mostly conservative, Edwards felt that he was sometimes too wavering on his opinions for the sake of peace in the House. He decided to wait until he had secured more support for his resolution before approaching him.

And then there was John Campbell, from Louisiana. They had sat at the same table over lunch several times, and he was certain that he was a good prospect for backing his ideas. Chris picked up the phone again and placed a call. "Congressman Campbell's office. May I help you?" A staff assistant answered the telephone. "Yes, this is Chris Edwards. Is Congressman Campbell available?" he asked. "Just one moment, and I'll put him on." She put the congressman on hold and Congressman Campbell answered the call a few moments later. "I'd be glad to," he said when Edwards asked if he was open for dinner. After hanging up, Chris hastily prepared a few notes to share with his colleague.

When Chris walked into the cafeteria, the older congressman was already waiting. The two placed their orders and sat down together. "What's on your mind?" Campbell asked him as they ate. So many thoughts were going on in Chris' mind that he didn't know where to begin. "I came to Washington thinking that I could actually make a difference with my work as a congressman," he began. "But during this time I have seen so much corruption; not just in Washington, but all over the entire nation, that I wasn't ever aware of." The other congressman knew there was something else Edwards was leading up to. "Have you ever wondered what would happen if our nation returned to the Judeo-Christian principles it was founded on?" Campbell stopped eating at his colleague's last statement. "This wasn't just a passing thought, was it?" he asked Edwards. "At first I thought that it was," Chris responded. "But I've not been able to get it out of my mind." He paused to take a drink from his glass.

"If you're expecting me to be shocked, I've been here for a long time. Nothing could surprise me at this point," the senior congressman assured Edwards. But Chris' reply did come as a surprise. "I'm really serious about this," he said. "We're watching the nation go down the drain, and doing absolutely nothing." He leaned forward as he continued spilling his thoughts. "I think we should put this question on the House floor." The older congressman almost choked and covered his mouth to keep from spitting his drink across the table. "So, what do you think?" Chris asked him. "If I understand correctly that you want to make this epiphany of yours into some sort of official resolution, I think it would be laughed off the floor," he responded. "That is, if the committee even allowed it to go that far." Congressman Campbell stood up and picked up his plate. "You can hang yourself if you want to, but I'm not holding the rope." He turned and left the table.

Edwards took a deep breath as he watched his colleague turn his tray in and walk out of the cafeteria. *"Maybe it's just not meant to be,"* he thought to himself. *"I just hope he'll forget what I said and not share it with anyone else."* His greatest fear was of becoming the laughing stock of the entire House of Representatives. The congressman finished eating his lunch, humiliated, before returning to his office.

4

Christianity Under Fire

Morning session was scheduled to begin in less than thirty minutes. Chris Edwards walked hastily through the Rotunda of the main Capitol Building and entered the Lower House Chamber. The freshman congressman wanted to arrive in enough time to review today's session agenda thoroughly. He also hoped to feel one or two other constituents out to see how many might be willing to listen to his ideas. But then, he wondered if anyone would even come close to him for fear of losing their voters' support once they found out what was on his mind.

Religion was a controversial topic all over the nation, especially in Washington. Others had tried unsuccessfully to challenge a number of the Supreme Court's rulings on the separation of Church and State, in attempts to return Christian values into the public arena. Edwards dared to believe that one day the country would reach the point that offending God was more important than offending the few who wished to take God out of America. The congressman knew that it would not be an overnight battle. He sat down at his desk in the chamber, pulled the agenda from his planner, and scanned through it briefly.

As he read the notes, he raised his eyebrows, wondering if he was seeing correctly. The first item, House Resolution 291 was a proposal to expand the nation's hate crime laws that would impose penalties on Christian nonprofits; even Churches and their pastors, if found to be discriminating against anyone based on-other-than Christian religious beliefs, sexual orientation or gender identity. It would also include penalties for openly criticizing others who lived together outside of marriage. This would put Christians and Churches in jeopardy if they openly mentioned the biblical teaching on adultery, fornication, or homosexual relationships. The bill was sponsored by Sara Jackson, a Progressive Party representative from Nevada; the congresswoman was a known atheist who held a strong influence over the Senate. She viciously fought against any bill having even the slightest hint of compassion toward Christian beliefs. CE-5 It was unthinkable that the House would consider making it a crime for pastors to preach anything in the Bible that might potentially offend anyone. No doubt, her bill had been inspired by the lawsuit against the city of San Esteban, CA by the San Esteban Association of Christian Churches. But Edwards couldn't understand why she would be pushing this before a ruling from the nation's high court was handed down. John Campbell stopped at his desk and said, "Hey, Edwards, did you see item one on the agenda?" He looked up and responded, "I'm reading it right now. I can hardly believe it! So, what do you think?" He knew the older congressman would be paying close attention to the proposed resolution, especially since they had been discussing a resolution that was its exact opposite.

"Coming from Sara, it's not at all surprising to me," Campbell replied. She was known as the "mother of all liberals," because of her radical platform. Very few thought that she could have been elected without the support of the liberal media. "I expect that the Speaker will throw it right to the judiciary subcommittee on the Constitution, where it will stay buried for months," the Louisiana representative mused. The sound of a gavel being struck on the desk echoed throughout the chamber, indicating the start of the morning session. Congressman Edwards turned and hurried to his seat.

"Ladies and gentlemen, let us come to order," the Speaker of the House addressed the assembly. He stood still for a moment to allow the congressmen to find their seats and get settled and then continued. "Let us bow our heads for the invocation." He stepped back to make room for the Chaplain of the House to address the body. Chaplain Peter Cartwright walked up to the podium at the front of the chamber and invited the assembly to join him in prayer. "Dear Lord," he opened his prayer. "May we always remember that righteousness exalts a nation, but sin is a disgrace to any people." All of those who had already reviewed the agenda took note of his prayer that seemed to address the new bill on their agenda, even though the chaplain never knew what was on the agenda before offering the invocation. It was always written in advance so it could be included in the daily journal. The chaplain asked for Divine guidance over each congressman in their deliberations, and concluded his prayer. After reciting the Pledge of Allegiance, the assembly was seated. "You have before you H.R. 291," the Speaker of the House announced, opening the morning business session. "Representative Sara Jackson has the floor to introduce its contents to the House."

The congresswoman was already standing. "Thank you, Mr. Speaker," she addressed Congressman Wilson. "Ladies and gentlemen of the House, I submit for your consideration House Resolution 291. Its purpose is to expand our nation's hate crime laws," there was an audible groan from both parties. "To include Christian nonprofits, Churches, and their leaders." The congresswoman spent the next three minutes outlining the major points of her resolution and then concluded her introduction. As Edwards looked around, he noted several representatives openly ignoring her speech. One congressman in front of him read a newspaper lying open on his desk. But Edwards felt he had a responsibility to listen to her presentation so he could give an honest review to his constituents, even though he already opposed it. The congresswoman completed the summary of her bill. Now it would be delegated to the rules committee for further review before sending it back to the House for debate. The morning session passed quickly, and the representatives adjourned for lunch.

After they reached the cafeteria, Edwards and John Campbell sat at a table off in the corner. "So what do you make of Sara's introduction to her bill?" He quizzed the older congressman. "I don't think it has a chance." "Neither do I," the senior replied. "But she's counting on next year being mid-term election year. Even if it fails, her supporters will remember that she introduced a bill that supports their sentiments. So it may be tougher than we're thinking. What about your proposal?" he asked. Chris was surprised when Campbell mentioned it because of his previous reaction at their last meeting. He hadn't expected the older representative to show any more interest in his idea unless he brought it back up. "If you're asking me to join you on this, I must say that I still have some questions about how it would affect my credibility," he said, trying not to sound uninterested. "I must have had you pegged wrong," Chris started to stand up, but the older congressman held up his hand. "Just do me a favor," he said in a softer tone. "Develop your ideas so I can see it first." He felt guilty for responding in such a direct manner and wanted the junior congressman to know that he was open to his idea, no matter how radical it might appear to be. After all, he remembered being in Edward's place as a younger congressman with the same high aspirations that his junior now expressed. "Narrow your thoughts to one or two specific goals," the congressman suggested.

Chris remained quiet for a moment before his response. "I'm thinking," he said slowly, "of a resolution that would restore the nation to strong economic policy, good moral values, and," he paused, "accountability of our leadership to the people." Congressman Campbell smiled. "That's something I believe I can stand with you on." Congressman Edwards was elated by his colleague's positive response. "Give me a few more days and I'll have it on your desk," he promised. He didn't want to tell John that he wanted to spend some time praying about his draft. After finishing their lunch, the two congressmen returned to their offices; both looked forward to see how Edwards' new concept would play out.

Later that day, the House adjourned after a lively debate, and Chris Edwards hurried back to his office. The congressman could hardly wait to hear back from his pastor in South Carolina and called his number as soon as he was back at his desk.

Scott Crawford had just returned to his office from a hospital visit and was starting on some miscellaneous tasks when his telephone rang. "Hello," he answered the phone. "Scott," Congressman Edwards greeted the pastor. "How are things going with you?" The pastor was thrilled to hear from the congressman. "It's been quite interesting lately, but I'm sure your work is more exciting," he replied. He was anxious to hear of any progress on the congressman's proposed bill. "I called to give you a quick update." The congressman began sharing what had transpired between himself and Congressman Campbell. "Well, you didn't get this far in your work without some opposition," Scott commented on his update. "You're bound to have some more once your proposal hits the house floor." Edwards fully expected a struggle just to get his ideas to the floor. Scott sensed that the congressman may be feeling some hesitancy because of this. "Just remember what God told Jeremiah when he commissioned him. *'Do not be afraid of them, for I am with you and will rescue you.'*" [13]   These were some words that the congressman needed to hear; he knew his call was providential. Before hanging up, the two agreed to meet again in the near future.

After pulling into the parking lot of their condo, Chris Edwards walked through the door to the smell of lasagna drifting from the kitchen. After another strenuous day, he was ready to spend some time with his sons and hear about their activities while he and Nancy were visiting in Blue Ridge Heights. Sixteen year old Justin was already a running back for his high school football team. Jamie was right behind him. He was expected to become kicker for the varsity team in the upcoming school term. Chris and Nancy were both proud of their sons and in spite of both of their heavy responsibilities, always found time to spend with them each week. They talked nearly the entire supper about their sports involvement. Pre-season training was starting the following week, and they were expected to meet after school for weight-lifting three days each week.

The teens were at the age where they were beginning to branch out in search of more independence. Chris and Nancy allowed them to grow but still expected them to live by a strict curfew of 9:00 during the week, and 10:00 on weekends, *if* they in fact, had a good reason to be gone. Sometimes this frustrated Justin and Jamie, because many of their friends were allowed to stay out much later. But the Edwards' believed that teens had no business staying out all hours of the night. They were more lenient with their time constraints on special occasions, so long as there was adequate adult supervision. After supper, they all helped clear the table, and then the two boys returned to their rooms to complete their homework.

Chris sat down in his recliner and picked up a legal pad lying on the lamp table next to his chair. He wanted to develop his thoughts on his proposed resolution in a logical manner. *"Proposed Bill...Give name for development,"* was scribbled across the top. Underneath was his list of objectives: "1. Strong economic policy, 2. Good moral values, and 3. Accountability of leaders." But the congressman still struggled about where his thoughts were leading to. *"Will this be a simple resolution, or should it call for a constitutional amendment?"* he wondered. It was probably still premature to be thinking about. He could already hear Congresswoman Jackson in his mind, protesting that this resolution would violate the Constitution. But Thomas Jefferson himself, the third President of the United States, had actually endorsed weekly worship services that were held in the House Chambers, sitting under preachers from a variety of Christian denominations. [14] "How could that be disputed, coming from the man who had written the phrase, *"a wall of the separation of Church and State?* [15]

Nancy walked in the living room, noticing her husband was in deep thought. "What are you working on?" she asked. Chris looked up and hesitated. "You may think that I've lost it," he told his wife. "Try me," she replied. Nancy never doubted her husband. He began to share the thoughts that had been on his mind for the past two weeks. "I'm beginning to question my own sanity," he said, as he finished telling his wife about the resolution. Nancy was flooded with pride as Chris shared his ideas which would more than likely have him labeled a "nut" if he presented it to his colleagues. This was the man she married; he had not strayed from his personal morals in spite of the enormous pressure from so many special interest groups that constantly petitioned his office. "If you feel strongly about this, then do it with no apology," she said. She knew that such a bill as what her husband was thinking could destroy even the best of congressmen. Chris jotted a few more thoughts down, and finally put his pad away, ready to rest for the evening.

About the same time, Scott and Connie Crawford were having a catch-up with their own children around their dining room table. As they ate, Scott thought it would be a good time to ask about their school lessons. "Have you noticed anything out of the ordinary in any of your classes?" Jordan looked up. "Well, we did start a new unit about world religions, he started. "We talked about Christianity, Islam, and Judaism." Both Scott and Connie were ready to learn more from their son's experience in this class, and Brianna seemed interested in the topic as well. "We spent a lot more time on Islam than Christianity," he continued. "So what did you learn?" Connie asked. "Well, when we were told to memorize the Five Pillars of Islam," Jordan paused, "I didn't think it was right, because we were not even allowed to discuss the Ten Commandments."

Scott was already disturbed by some of the same things that Lucas had already shared with him. "Is there anything else you think we should know?" Scott questioned his son further. Jordan was a little uneasy about saying more on the topic but the conversation had already started, so he opened up. "Mrs.

Crenshaw also said that Christianity was becoming hostile toward Islam and Muslims in general," he said. Although troubled by what his son had just said, the pastor was careful not to show his feelings. He was quiet for a moment. "Did I say something wrong?" Jordan asked his father. "Not at all," Scott replied. "It's good that you don't feel right about what you were told. I've heard the same thing from someone else. I think it's something we need to talk with the principal about." Chris promised Jordan that he would be discreet when he talked to the school officials. "I think that you'll see you're not alone in this one," he assured his son.

Lucas had just pulled out a cart at the grocery store when he spotted Kelly Graham, the president of the local PTA. The two exchanged casual greetings as they met each other. Lucas had already planned to give Kelly a call, so he decided to go ahead and mention his concerns. "When is your next meeting?" he asked. Kelly was surprised at the question, because he had never shown any interest in the PTA. She still appreciated his interest. "Two weeks from Thursday," she replied. "Do you have a specific concern, or just interested in meeting the group?" Lucas was wondering about the best way to bring up his concerns, and Kelly had opened the door. "I was speaking with my pastor earlier," he told her. "He suggested that I talk with you." Kelly pulled her cart over to the side of the aisle to stay out of the other shoppers' way. "The other day I was going over a study guide with my daughter, Emily," the single father started. "The lesson was about World Religions." Kelly instantly knew what he was talking about. Another parent had already approached her, but she was interested in hearing Lucas' story, so she didn't interrupt.

"Why are other religions being promoted while ignoring our own beliefs?" he asked the PTA president. "A lot of people believe that it is a part of the standardized curriculum that many states have adopted," she responded. "That's too early to know for sure, but I think one of the reasons is that educators from other faiths have been more open about their own beliefs; and some Christian teachers feel pressure to steer away from the Christian aspect for fear of causing conflict." She assured Lucas that this would be a topic of heavy discussion at the upcoming meeting; Lucas assured her that he would make plans to be there.

While a storm was brewing on the campus of Blue Ridge Heights Academy in the foothills of South Carolina, another cloud was looming above King University, a Christian College just over 100 miles away, in Charlotte. Dr. David Gambrell, the President of King University was a native of Blue Ridge Heights, and had also been raised at the Trinity Christian Fellowship where he attended until he left for college many years ago. He was married to his high school sweetheart for 25 years, but she had died two years earlier after a long battle with cancer. Now, Dr. Gambrell poured his heart into his work as president of the school. King University had recently celebrated its centennial anniversary, and boasted an enrollment of nearly 4,000 students. But even more than their enrollment, the university prided itself as being a school that commanded excellence in every major of study they offered.

Its prestige didn't come without controversy, however. The university identified itself as an independent Bible-believing school. It firmly adhered to a system of strict standards in spite of the fact that most Christian schools were more relaxed in their individual discipline. And they did so unapologetically. Dr. Gambrell, on occasion, reminded his students that they didn't expect the students to live by every rule in the book after they graduated from the university. The purpose of these strict standards was to prepare their students to live more balanced lives once they entered into the real world.

The university president was preparing to visit his hometown for a short break in a few more days, and hoped to visit his old Church during his visit. Today, he planned to focus on a long list of things that had piled up over the past several weeks. He took a stack of mail from his secretary as he walked into his office, laid the envelopes on his desk, and sat down to clear his mind before starting his day. An envelope addressed to him, and headed with the name, *Society for Alternative Living* caught his attention. He slowly opened the envelope, bracing himself for what the latest attack would be. The letter read:

> Dr. Gambrell,
> This is to inform you that the Society for Alternative
> Living is planning a march in front of King University
> in the near future to protest its discriminating
> policies against the Alternative Living community.
> I look forward to seeing you there.
> Until we overcome,
> Marcus Jefferson.

Dr. Gambrell leaned forward and put his face into his hands, taking a deep breath. In his mind, the president could see the former student gloating at the opportunity to attack the school. At first the school's administration had hoped that this would be a short-lived protest by a few disgruntled alumni, but it was becoming clear that it might turn into an extended battle. He leaned back and logged onto his computer. After the screen lit up he began composing a letter.

To the members of the board,
I regret to have to inform you of a conflict that
has arisen involving King University. Several
Alumni of the school have joined together
under the leadership of Marcus Jefferson, (also
a former student) as a unique branch of the
National Association for Social Equality.
Its purpose is to defame the name of the school,
and force it to compromise our biblical
standards of living. I will keep you posted
on this situation as it continues to develop.
In His Victory,
David Gambrell

Since his secretary had just left for the day, Dr. Gambrell made several copies of the letter and prepared to send them out himself.

Emily Hall slid her tray down the rail on the serving line in the school cafeteria, and pulled out some change to pay for her lunch. She nearly bumped into Brianna, one of her closest friends, as she turned around to find an empty seat. "Oops!" she exclaimed, struggling to keep from spilling her food tray all over the floor. "Oh, hey there," Brianna said when she saw her. The two girls spotted an empty table nearby and sat down to eat lunch together. "So, how did your spring break go?" Emily asked. "Boring," she replied, chewing her food. "Grandpa doesn't do internet, and we were so far out in the country, my cell-phone wouldn't even work," she smiled. *"No Way!"* Emily exclaimed. "What did you do all day?" she asked. "Most of the time, we just sat around and watched TV. But we did get to ride the horses. Staying in the country has its benefits. So what about you?" she asked her friend. "We just stayed in town. Nothing that interesting to talk about," Emily replied.

"Oh, did your parents tell you about the visitors in Church?" she asked Brianna. "They said that some congressman and his wife were here for a weekend visit." She paused a moment. "Yeah, Chris and Nancy Edwards. It feels weird, calling a friend by their first name, and then they become famous," Emily mused. "Mom said we should call him 'congressman,' out of respect." "I suppose she's right," Brianna said. "Mama said they have two sons, but they weren't there. What about them?" She wanted to learn more about the congressman's teen sons. "They're twins, and 16 years old; and they're so cute!" Brianna giggled. "Maybe they'll come back if their parents visit again?" she speculated.

They ate in silence for a moment. "Oh, I meant to ask, what did your dad say about Mrs. Crenshaw's assignment?" Emily asked. "I think he wants to find out more about it," Brianna replied. "He's not opposed to us being exposed to other religions, but he doesn't think the school should go into other religion's beliefs, without allowing our own beliefs to be discussed." The two girls were silent for a moment as they continued eating. "What about Jordan? Did he get in trouble for getting into it with Mrs. Crenshaw? You should've been there!" Emily was impressed that Jordan had stood up to the teacher. "I'm sure she won't hold it against him," Brianna responded, smiling. But she may not be so lucky with the school district." The bell rang before she could finish her thought. The two friends carried their empty trays up to the window where the dishes were washed and then parted to go to their own classrooms.

64

5

Establishing Alliances

Senator Roger Francis walked down the corridor leading to his office suite. It had been a long day already, although it was only half way through. His schedule had doubled with the added responsibilities of preparing for the upcoming presidential debates and other public events. The senator had just met with his campaign manager who reported that he was soaring in the polls. But the introduction of H.R. 291 by Congresswoman Jackson had complicated his campaign. After weeks of preparing for his scheduled debates, the senator felt prepared for his first appearance. But her radical proposal was certain to affect the direction in which his first debate would go. He also needed a clear plan of how to respond to any questions by the media on where he stood regarding her proposed bill. It was the perfect dilemma for even the most seasoned lawmaker's race. He must be careful how he verbalized his opinion about this bill. While he was opposed to any measure that would threaten the institution of religious freedom, it might cost him the election if he went against her resolution. The senator sat down and placed a call to his publicist.

Work at the UBC Studios in Washington was becoming more intense with the presidential elections drawing nearer, along with the social issues creating so much unrest around the country. Marvin Maddox walked through the entrance to the broadcasting studio and down the main hallway. The anchorman had been in an extended conference with his producer and was in a rush to get his program lined up for the evening news. Now, he entered the room where the news program would begin in less than twenty minutes. The ceiling was filled with spotlights. Several large flat screens lined the walls on each side of the platform the anchor's desk sat on. A camera man was already in the room turning his equipment on.

The middle aged, graying anchorman sat down behind his desk and looked up when he saw Harold Gentry, the news director entering the room. "I just sent a new item to your computer. We need to discuss it before the program begins," he informed Marvin hurriedly. "I'm just getting here, so I'll take a look as soon as I get my system turned on," the anchor responded. "Fill me in while I get settled."

Harold leaned over the anchor's desk. "We just received the daily report from the Capitol," he informed Marvin. "A new bill has been presented in the House of Representatives by Sara Jackson. It's the biggest news we've received from the House in weeks." Marvin turned on the monitor that was inlaid into his report desk and began scrolling through the reports to locate the story Harold was talking about. "Oh, and don't comment on that Church case at the Supreme Court today. That might bring too much attention to either issue, since they're somewhat related." The director turned and left the room just as quickly as he had entered.

Marvin enjoyed his job as evening anchor for UBC, but he felt pressured to ignore news items that reflected the

66

conservative population in a positive light. It seemed as if his job was to support the liberal political agenda. This frustrated the anchorman, because it went against his journalistic philosophy to simply report the facts. He hastily scanned through each story as the room began to fill with the production crew before air time.

The principal of Blue Ridge Heights Academy sat at his desk preparing the morning announcements. Steve Williams was in his early 30s, with wavy brown hair. He was an avid athlete, and didn't shy away from a game of basketball with his young students during the daily recess. The principal who was also the youth pastor at Trinity Christian Fellowship, had come there just a year before Scott Crawford had been called as its pastor. He was a natural communicator with his students. Although he was careful to keep his work as a youth pastor separate from his weekly role of principal, he was fondly referred to as "Pastor Steve" by many of his students.

The telephone rang in his office and he paused from his scribbling in some changes in the announcements. "Steve Williams speaking," he answered the call. "Oh, yes?" He continued when Scott Crawford spoke to him. "I'm not trying to add to your list of complaints," the pastor told him, "but you should be aware of an issue that has several parents concerned." He had the principal's full attention. "Tell me about it," he replied. "This one's going to be touchy," Scott said, hesitating. "It involves Karen Crenshaw. She's Jordan and Brianna's History teacher, and several others from our Church," The principal continued listening as he took notes on a pad. "One of her recent classes may have overstepped the bounds of religious instruction," he informed the principal. Although Steve and his pastor had a good working relationship, he tried to be careful in response to Scott's concerns. "In her defense, this is part of the curriculum, and she is obligated to present it to the students."

"We don't have a problem teaching *about* the religion," the pastor responded. "That's a necessary part of understanding the various cultures. But I do have a problem with other religious beliefs being taught when the tenets of Christianity aren't even brought up." Steve felt the same way as his pastor. "If she is presenting any content to the exclusion of another religion, I was unaware of it," he told his pastor. "One of the parents may bring it up at the PTA meeting next week," he informed the principal. "You may want to be there to clarify the issue." Steve told him he would plan on attending the meeting. He also gave his assurance that he would address the topic in a faculty meeting before the PTA meeting. Pastor Scott agreed to be there to lend his support as well.

Back on Capitol Hill, Congressman Edwards had been developing some more thoughts for his resolution for several weeks. He had the prospect of strong support from both Congressmen Campbell and the Speaker of the House. Before he went to Senator Smith, he had to be sure. Even though he was well qualified for his work as a congressman, he still felt encouraged after meeting, and confiding with Scott Crawford nearly a month ago. He was anxious to discuss the latest developments in the Congressional House with his pastor. Since Nancy's work schedule did not permit her to accompany him, he decided to make a quick run back to Blue Ridge Heights alone. It was nearly 4:30 in the afternoon when the congressman drove his rented car into the small town, so he decided to go directly to the Church to see if Scott was still in his office. The pastor's car was still in the parking lot when the Church building came into sight, so he stopped. Scott was pleasantly surprised to see the congressman walk in.

"You've been on my mind all day," the pastor greeted him. "I can hardly wait to hear about the progress on your resolution." Edwards smiled, knowing that someone was genuinely interested in his proposal. "It's had a slow start," the congressman admitted. "But we have a working outline. After we get some more participation on the House level, I'll send it over to Senator Smith for his input. He will be a key player in gaining support on his end." Scott agreed with him.

"There's something else that you may have already heard on the news," Edwards said, leaning forward in his chair. "The day after I returned from my last visit, Sara Jackson introduced a bill that, if passed could be a threat to the entire Christian Community." This was the first time Scott had heard about this. "I haven't watched too much TV since then. Tell me about it." Edwards gave him a brief summary of what the bill included. "I really can't say it's that much of a surprise," Scott replied, "especially since our nation has continued to embrace more and more ungodly morals over the last several years," He understood the implications this law could have on his Church if it were actually passed.

Neither of the two men spoke for a moment, reflecting on the seriousness of the situation. "From a pastor's point of view, it's most distressing to see America throwing our Christian beliefs out the door by the day. Maybe the Lord has allowed you to be in the place you're at today to turn these things around," Scott suggested. "Yes, but how?" Edwards asked thoughtfully.

"Do you know the Chaplain of the House?" the pastor asked. "Peter Cartwright? I've never met him personally; but I see him when he opens up the morning sessions with prayer." the congressman responded. "Since your bill addresses spiritual concerns, he would be a strong ally. He can't vote, but he will give you his prayerful support." Congressman Edwards wondered why he had never thought of this idea. *"He would be an ally,"* he thought silently. It was getting late by this time, so the two men prayed together for Divine guidance as Congressman Edwards moved ahead with his bill. The young politician was spending the night at his mother's house. The next day, he would meet with Brad at his State office before returning to Washington.

After returning to the Capitol, Congressman Edwards headed toward his office in the Rayburn House Office Building. Several fellow lawmakers were sitting in a lounge watching a flat screened television on the wall. President William Duncan had just approached the podium in an unexpected news-conference. Edwards stepped into the room to listen.

"Ladies and gentlemen of the press, thank you for joining me on such a short notice. I would like to comment on the bill submitted to the House by Congresswoman Sara Jackson. H.R. 291 asks for Congress to clearly define any verbal expression against minorities, such as the alternate living community as hate speech. Our society must not put up with intolerance, hate or discrimination. Criticizing these people, just because we don't agree with or understand them must not be allowed." The President paused to take a brief look at his notes. "When this nation was founded the dominant religion was Christianity, but its founders never intended to rule out any other religion. Over the last several decades, some of the teachings within the Christian community have become hostile toward today's society. This hostility toward others they simply don't agree with must be stopped. And so I ask you to urge your congressmen to pass this bill."

70

President Duncan looked up from his podium and began taking questions from the press, but the lawmakers listening to the conference began talking excitedly. Even members of the Progressive Party were disturbed by the President's comments. *"We must not tolerate intolerance?"* one of the congressmen sputtered incredulously. The general consensus was that the President had overstepped his boundaries in his statement against the Christian population.

Congressman Edwards left the lounge with a churning feeling deep in his stomach. *"Has the Church become hostile to our society, or has our nation become hostile toward Christianity?"* he wondered. The counsel that Pastor Scott Crawford had given him was ringing through his ears, *"Leadership is doing what's right, only after much prayer, regardless of the consequences."* This recent turn of events affirmed his resolve to take his stand. He continued the short walk to his office and entered the reception area where Jessica was working in a nearby office. "I forwarded some calls to your voice mail," she said to Edwards as she walked out and handed a stack of mail to him. "Thank you, Jessica," he stopped to speak with his executive assistant. "I may be out for most of the afternoon, so you'll have the office to yourself." He continued into his office to begin catching up on his incoming correspondence.

Chaplain Peter Cartwright sat behind his desk working on his weekly Bible Study. The telephone rang, and he stopped writing to answer it. It was his administrative assistant. She announced that Congressman Edwards had arrived, and then ushered him into his office. The chaplain rose and walked around his desk to greet Edwards as he entered. "Good afternoon, congressman," he said warmly. He offered Chris a chair and sat down next to him. The chaplain had not met Edwards, and so he spent several minutes getting to know him. He considered the entire House of Representatives as his personal "flock" although it was a challenge to speak personally with each representative on a regular basis. He sensed genuineness in the younger congressman. *"A refreshing change,"* he thought quietly.

"How can I help you, today?" the chaplain always tried to help his visitors feel unrestricted in what, and how much they wanted to discuss with him. His relaxed disposition immediately put the congressman at ease, and he began to share his spiritual awakening with the chaplain.

"Everybody that comes to Washington has the same desire to make a difference," Chaplain Cartwright told him. "But no one has ever approached me with a passion to see America return to its moral values." "So what do you think?" Edwards asked the chaplain. "This is a confirmation to me," Cartwright responded slowly. "The same thing has been going through my own mind for weeks." He paused and then asked, "How much support, and how much opposition?" Congressman Edwards was thoughtful for a moment. "I have two other fellow representatives I think might be on board, and possibly one senator. The Senate could be the roadblock." The chaplain detected some uncertainty that Chris may be feeling about moving forward with the resolution. "Don't underestimate the power of bi-partisanship," he advised. Even though there's been so much gridlock over the past several years, some good things could come out of this if both parties catch the vision." The chaplain's counsel was an encouragement to Edwards. He had come, uncertain as to just what he was asking for; but Chaplain Cartwright gave him spiritual support, and some good thoughts on how to communicate with the opposition.

As their conversation came to an end, both men stood up, each wishing that this conversation could continue on. It was inspiring to be having a discussion that had no hint of discord, *"especially at the Capitol!"* Edwards thought. "There may be a strong fight," the chaplain cautioned him, and then added, "but if God is for us, who can be against us?" [16] The two men shook hands, and agreed to find a time to meet for prayer and fellowship in the near future.

Steve Williams sat down at the P.A. system in the main office of Blue Ridge Heights Academy. The bell would ring shortly, and he was rushing to squeeze all the announcements in. "Teachers," he started on the first item. "Remember, this month's faculty meeting will be this afternoon from 3:15 to 4:00." The bell cut him off before he could finish. The quiet hallway outside the office immediately awakened with the sounds of locker doors slamming shut and students rushing to get to their cars or buses. Mr. Williams stepped back into his office to relax for a few more minutes before the faculty meeting began. He would go on to the library as soon as the student traffic had died down.

Students in the library rushed out of the room when the final bell rang; the few who remained hastily checked out their books before leaving. The librarian rolled a media cart near an open wall. This area was used for faculty meetings, and she needed to make sure the equipment was working properly in case Mr. Williams needed it for an overhead presentation. The sound of students in the halls gradually faded, replaced by more activity in the library as the teachers began assembling around the tables. Karen Crenshaw was among the last to arrive for the meeting, in hopes she wouldn't be asked any more questions by her associates wondering why she was under fire from so many parents.

A few minutes later Mr. Williams entered the library and stood behind the podium. "I know your time is valuable, so I'll take care of this business as quickly as I can," the principal addressed his teachers. He held a stack of booklets entitled, *"A Teacher's Guide to Religion in the Public Schools,"* and handed them to the librarian to pass around to the faculty. "The first thing I'd like to discuss is our policy on addressing religion in the classroom," he continued. "You should already be familiar with this policy, but since there have been some recent questions, maybe we should take a quick review." Although Steve was a good communicator, he was struggling with his words. His personal Christian beliefs were not the issue; but the potential conflict involving one of his teachers and several students, all of which were members of his Church, forced him to proceed cautiously. The meeting passed without any questions or comments about the policy. But the teachers knew that the issue would probably resurface at the upcoming PTA meeting.

Chris Edwards inserted a folder into his brief case and left his office. He had worked for the last hour to revise an outline for his thoughts that Congressman Campbell had suggested. Before speaking to any other lawmakers for their support, he needed to be sure he had one strong ally on his side. He left the office and began walking toward the cafeteria where he and Campbell usually met. Lunch was not yet being served when he reached the dining commons, but he could still discuss his proposal to the senior representative while they waited.

He laid the folder on the table next to Campbell and then sat down. The older congressman tilted his glasses lower on his nose so he could read the contents of the folder. "You've been doing some serious work on this since we talked," he commented. "Nice outline, but do you have any thoughts on how you will publicize it?" Chris rubbed his chin thoughtfully. "I've not given much thought to that at all," he said. "Don't worry," Campbell looked over Chris' resolution draft for a moment. "Let's get it to the floor first; its identity will come naturally." Chris waited for the other congressman's opinion on his work. Now that he had thrown his hat over the fence, he would have to stick with it. There was no turning back, now.

"It's a very noble proposal," the older congressman told Edwards. "But it still needs a lot of work. Before taking it to the floor you need more support than you already have. Many a good resolution has died before it ever hit the hopper for lack of adequate backing," he cautioned his junior associate. "So, you think it has a chance?" Chris was excited that his mentor was taking the time to critique. "Like I said, it has some excellent points, but good intentions won't necessarily get it passed." Edwards sat in silence. Congressman Campbell sensed his discouragement. Maybe he had gone too hard? "I tell you what," he proposed. "There are several other representatives who are discussing some similar thoughts. I think yours would go along very well." Edwards' face lit up. He hadn't heard of another resolution even remotely close to his, but he wanted to learn more.

As Congressman Edwards was leaving the cafeteria, Senator Hudson and Representative Graham Gillespie, another freshman congressman from Alabama were walking in his direction. "I've been hoping to hear from you," the senator greeted Edwards. "Congressman Campbell was telling me about a piece of legislation you've been working on. I'd like to know more about it." Edwards didn't want to ruin this opportunity to gain another supporter. He followed them back into the cafeteria and again, joined Congressman Campbell. Chris pulled his resolution proposal out as he sat down, anxious to see what the

75

other two lawmakers would say. "So," Senator Hudson began to talk, "What can you tell us about it?"

Congressman Edwards cleared his throat nervously. A new thought had just entered his mind. "I'm thinking about labeling it *The Moral and Ethics Accountability Act,"* he said quickly. "Hmmm, it sounds more like a revolution to me," Congressman Gillespie piped in. "It could be?" Edwards smiled. "Give us a quick breakdown of your thoughts," Senator Hudson sounded interested. "My thoughts are to create a standard by which both the House and Senate will restore the nation to its moral values; this will mandate a reform of our economic policy, leadership accountability and of the judicial system." He cleared his throat again while waiting for someone to break the silence. "It's an interesting idea, especially with a focus on such major changes in Washington," the senator said as he glanced through the notes. "But I'm with you. We need to work harder to challenge the status quo in Washington."

Congressman Gillespie leaned forward thoughtfully. "I think it would be a tremendous addition to the one we've already got in the pot," he proposed. Chris was elated. "Tell me about yours," he said. "The idea we've been talking about would actually propose several constitutional amendments," Hudson explained. "It will more than likely turn into a joint resolution. Go ahead, John," the senator turned toward Congressman Campbell. "The first amendment would impose term limits on the House and Senate," John Campbell spoke up. He was watching the other three to see how they were thinking. "The next item would be aimed at restoring judicial accountability and integrity. One major part of this amendment would be to impose a term limit of one ten year period in the Supreme Court." Campbell paused momentarily as two members of the

Progressive Party passed by their table. He didn't want the resolution to become public until it had become more defined.

"So what do you think?" He asked Edwards. Chris was excited about the new ideas, and expressed his sentiments. It confirmed that he wasn't alone. However, something was still missing. "Let's find at least two congressmen from the Progressive party who might be willing to join us," Senator Hudson suggested. "Then you'll have a stronger chance at getting it passed on the floor. Meanwhile, I'll be talking around with a few senators. It'll take awhile to get your points whittled out, and if we get some buzz going in the Senate, it will stand a better chance of passing on this end." he concluded. The four legislators brought their meeting to a close as the other congressmen around them began leaving the cafeteria, signaling the afternoon session was nearing.

6

No Compromises

Mrs. Crenshaw's students were quiet as she recorded the topic each one had chosen for their research paper. "Mr. Crawford," the history teacher smiled at Jordan. "Yes ma'am," he responded. "I'm doing my paper on how Christianity shaped the early history of the United States." Jordan's classmates were restless from the long wait to give their report topic to the teacher. But they were fully awake when they heard him announce the subject he had chosen. "I'm sorry, but you'll have to choose another topic," Mrs. Crenshaw said abruptly. "There will be no research with any religious content in this class." [17]

Everyone's eyes were glued on their classmate to see his response. He didn't look up. "I'll have to think of something else," he replied to his teacher, humiliated by her denial. Mrs. Crenshaw was a well-liked teacher, but her antagonistic treatment toward Jordan was causing her to lose their respect. The class was unusually quiet for the rest of the period. Mrs. Crenshaw sensed her students' cold disapproval of her action, and dismissed the class a few minutes early to go home for the day.

Late in the afternoon, Chris Edwards was preparing to leave his office for the day when a knock came at his door. John Campbell appeared. "Come in," Edwards welcomed him. Very rarely did other congressmen come by his office unless there was a piece of legislation that needed some support. There was a tense expression on his face. "Have a seat," Edwards motioned toward a table in the corner of his office, and they sat down together. "Chris," the older congressman said slowly. "I just wanted to give you a head's up on the pending Jackson Bill," he told his younger counterpart. Chris looked up, unsure of what the other lawmaker was about to say. "The Rules Committee has approved amendments to the bill that will provide more severe penalties for Churches who violate the proposed bill. This would include loss of tax exempt status, and possible loss of property. This could even affect individual members as well." Chris tried to process what he had just heard quietly for a few moments. "So, just what would qualify for these penalties?" he finally asked. "All it would take is to openly criticize anyone's personal or religious beliefs, even though the views are based on biblical teaching." CE-6 Edwards felt the all-too familiar tension welling up inside.

"How can this motion even being considered?" Congressman Edwards showed his frustration. "The Association for Social Equality has been hammering both parties pretty hard," Congressman Campbell explained. "But that violates the free-speech clause," Edwards protested. "I know. But it will be open for debate at the start of next week's session." Chris Edwards was still visibly disturbed. It almost seemed as if from the time he had started on his own measures and began having a personal time of prayer each day for the country, an evil floodgate had been opened. America had made some very open moves away from Christian morals over the past several years. Now

80

legislation was being proposed to criminalize the religious beliefs and teachings of Churches throughout America? He couldn't see how this resolution had even made it past the committee. But it would have to go through the proper procedure, and hopefully, the bill would be killed. "Let's just pray that it doesn't pass," Campbell said gravely, before standing up to leave.

On Thursday evening Lucas Hall turned into the parking lot at the Blue Ridge Heights Academy. He was surprised to see so many cars there, because Kelly had mentioned that there was little participation in their school's chapter. The single father slipped into the cafeteria where the group had just opened the meeting. The room was packed with parents, students and teachers; all had shown up for the same reason that Lucas had come. As he looked around, he saw several other parents that he knew. Karen Crenshaw looked up with a cringe on her face when Lucas found a chair across the aisle from where she was seated.

"We have a few new faces tonight," Kelly announced, "and I would like to welcome you all. I want to begin with an issue that several people have approached me about. And I asked our principal, Steve Williams to be here so he can answer any questions you might have." Mr. Williams, who sat near the podium turned and raised his hand in appreciation for the parents' applause. "Several parents have spoken with me of their concerns about some of the lessons that have appeared in one of the classrooms this year," the PTA president announced. "This is a unit in World History on comparing world religions." Lucas couldn't read Mrs. Crenshaw's face, but the atmosphere seemed to turn an icy cold when the lesson was brought up. "Our children are not supposed to be given any religious preference whenever religion is brought up," she continued. "The concern is that this may have occurred during this unit." Mrs. Crenshaw stood up and interrupted Kelly. "I'm sure you all know that this took place in my class," the teacher said defensively. "But I've followed the curriculum," she firmly held her ground.[18]

Kelly paused uncomfortably before she resumed talking. "I don't think there's a problem with discussing, or even comparing the different religious beliefs. We just need to know if our children have been taught this in any way that might put any religion above another-specifically our own Christian convictions." One mother sitting near the front raised her hand. "My son showed me the worksheet," she said. "It required him to write down and memorize the Five Pillars of Islam. I'd like to know why the Ten Commandments weren't on that study guide." "Or Jesus' Beattitudes," someone across the room added. The history teacher was still standing and responded quickly. "The law is clear about that," she said. "The Supreme Court has ruled that the Ten Commandments cannot be taught, or displayed in any public school setting." She was sure that he had put this issue to an end, but the teacher wasn't out of the hot seat yet. Pastor Scott Crawford was standing behind her, waiting to be recognized to speak.

"Rev. Crawford, it's good to have you with us tonight," Kelly acknowledged the pastor, giving him a nod to speak. "Thank you, Kelly," he responded to her recognition. "The very mention of religion, especially when it concerns the Bible is grossly misunderstood regarding its place in public schools." Scott turned to face the entire gathering. "Actually, The U.S. Supreme Court has ruled that public schools must not participate in *devotional* teaching of religion. The court stated that academic teaching *about* religion in the public classroom was not only constitutional, but needed." [19]   He paused as a murmur went around the room. "I understand that this subject has been addressed in a recent faculty meeting, and hopefully this was clarified." A healthy discussion continued after Scott returned to his seat.

Lucas was thankful that Scott commented on his own concerns. The pastor was more effective in verbalizing this matter. But he was glad just the same, that he had come to the meeting. And the presence of those who had come to speak up for these concerns was an encouragement to Kelly, as well. She had been facing increasing pressure from many parents to help resolve the division. It was good to know that she had some support, if it should become necessary to go further than tonight's meeting. As soon as there was a pause between those who had spoken for and against the classroom conflict, she changed the discussion to the next item on the agenda.

AJ Wilson sat at his desk scanning through the previous week's journal. The upcoming presidential race, coupled with the most recent resolution that Sara Jackson had presented was creating a logistical nightmare. His job was to put the bill with the most likelihood of success next in line for debate on the House floor. With the mid-term elections over, it was imperative that unity be restored in both houses, or the outcome of the next presidential election could be less than desired. A stack of proposals that needed to be sorted through lay on a small table next to his desk. Every piece of legislation presented from here on would be closely scrutinized by both political parties, and more importantly, a host of unsatisfied voters. Since H.R. 291 was highly unpopular with the ever growing conservative population, it was likely to be voted down in the House of Representatives.

The sound of several familiar voices speaking in the main forum of his office suite came from the other side of his closed door. Ordinarily he wouldn't have heard these voices until he was rang by Carolyn, his executive assistant; Wilson was a driven person that maintained a deep focus on whatever task he was engaged in, but with so much on his mind, today he was unable to concentrate. He stood and opened his door. Congressmen Edwards and Campbell were speaking to Carolyn. "Good afternoon, comrades," the Speaker greeted the congressmen and motioned for them to follow him into his office. A visit from two members of the House this time of day meant one of two things; either they had come to oppose a pending bill, or to present one of their own. He already had a full plate, so he was hoping that neither would be the case. "So, to what do I owe this occasion?" he asked as they were seated.

"We have a new resolution in the incubator. This one could raise more eyebrows than H.R. 291," Congressman Campbell answered his inquiry. "I'm almost afraid to ask, but let's hear about it," Congressman Wilson responded with interest. "Chris came to me with some ideas several weeks before number 291 was introduced to the House," Campbell continued. "His proposal is the total opposite of the Jackson Bill." He referred to the Congresswoman's resolution. "That should make for some interesting drama," the Speaker of the House mused. He dreaded another controversial debate. But he sat back and listened thoughtfully to the ideas that had almost possessed Congressman Edwards for the last several weeks.

"What makes this proposal stand out above the one that it opposes?" Congressman Wilson asked. "It wasn't intended to oppose HR 291," Edwards spoke up. "The Jackson bill was introduced just before Congressman Edwards decided to go public with his," John Campbell supported Edwards. "This bill does what no other resolution has proposed for many decades." He handed the Speaker a copy of the outline. "In short, it will

84

call for a complete ethics reform in all three branches of the federal government."

"Wait a minute." Wilson leaned forward in his chair. You actually believe this Congress is going to grow a conscience before the presidentials?" He was being facetious, yet serious at the same time. It would be political suicide to introduce such a proposition so close to the elections. "Absolutely," Congressman Edwards countered. "Just think about it," Campbell spoke up. "This resolution is just what the public wants to see," he defended the proposal. "America has a near zero confidence in Congress." Congressman Edwards sounded like a salesman ready to close. "Passing this bill would be a good start in restoring some respect."

The House Speaker stood up, closing his folder. "I'm due at another meeting in about five minutes," he said. "It sounds like a very risky proposition. But then again, anything the Constitution Party presents these days is risky." They chuckled at the Speaker's remark. "However, it might benefit our party," he added. "I'd like to see the full draft, if you can email me a copy." Both Campbell and Edwards stood and picked up their folders to leave. "There are several other congressmen with some similar ideas. I believe they would make an excellent resolution, if the two were merged together." Campbell was determined to finish what he had come to say. "Get me a copy of theirs and we'll look at them both." Wilson replied. The two shook the Speaker's hand as they walked into the hallway. They waited for him to disappear around the corner before picking up their conversation.

"If you have a few hours tomorrow, maybe we can meet with the others," Campbell suggested. "We can discuss both ideas, and perhaps get a good working resolution started. We need to get it to A.J. while it's fresh on his mind." Chris knew this may be a turning point in making his thoughts a reality, although he had been looking forward to the weekend after a pressing week. They agreed to meet in the morning in order to keep their afternoon free.

Russell Taylor stood behind the tiller in his garden turning the soil under. Since retiring, he had taken up his old love for gardening, and over the last growing season harvested enough fresh vegetables to last him and his wife, and daughter's family for another year. But he still wanted to remain active in his work for the Lord. The older minister looked up when he saw Ruby waving from the back porch to get his attention. He shut the engine down and headed toward the house. "Scott Crawford called a few minutes ago," his wife told him as he walked up the porch steps. "I told him I'd have you call him back." She handed him the telephone and walked back inside. Russell was ready for a break, and sat down to dial the younger minister's telephone number.

The Church office was quiet as Pastor Scott sat, reading over this week's sermon notes. The sound of his cell phone ringing broke the silence. He was delighted to hear Russell's voice on the other end. In the past it may have been a year or longer before they spoke to each other, but their communication had become quite regular over the last two months. Rev. Taylor was amazed that Scott was still seeing doors open for his ministry to Congressman Edwards. "So fill me in on the latest with your work," he said. "I don't know if this is progress, or a setback," Scott replied, and then began sharing the conflict involving the school and Jordan's teacher, who was also a church member. Then he explained how NASE was lobbying to influence Congress to vote for the anti-Christian legislation. "You know," Rev. Taylor sighed, "this immorality that the alternate living community is trying to impose on the majority of the nation could be the one polarizing issue that brings America back to its knees." The younger minister agreed. "Don't be surprised at what, or who you may encounter in your work," Russell counseled Scott. "When you invade the devil's territory, he will fight with any and every available tool he has at his disposal. But don't forget, prayer is a power that the enemy can never overcome."

Scott was encouraged by the older minister's words. If there were any doubts in his mind regarding his involvement in the school controversy, there was no doubt now. He had a responsibility to take a stand.

The offices at the UBC Headquarters had already emptied for the day, but the studio was still buzzing with activity. Marvin Maddox sat behind the anchor desk in the studio. It had been a stressful day, and his mind was on how he would spend the evening after wrapping up the final broadcast. Announcing the news was the easy part of his job. Having to communicate peacefully between himself, his news-editor, and the numerous others who contacted him throughout the week was the challenge. "Quiet on the set!" the news director announced sharply, directing his focus to the "On Air" light that was blinking above the door behind the camera man. "Three, two..." The theme music began playing, and the anchorman focused on the camera in front of his desk.

"Good evening, and welcome to the UBC Evening News from Washington," Maddox opened the news program. "The National Association for Social Equality, also known as NASE, has stepped up its pressure on Congress to pass House Resolution 291. If passed, this resolution could enact criminal penalties against pastors of local Churches *and their members*, if they were to openly criticize not just gays and lesbians, but even persons who have chosen to live in non-marital heterosexual relationships; what the Church commonly refers to as 'adultery,'" the anchorman announced. "The penalties could include loss of tax exempt status for Churches and Christian nonprofits, and conceivably, the loss of personal property. This bill has met vicious opposition from members of the Constitution Party. But tonight we will hear my recent interview of Darrell Youngblood, the President of NASE, to learn why they feel this should be made into law." Maddox had barely opened the evening program, and already had a bad feeling about the divisive proposal he had just announced. Was it just him, or did others see it as a danger to America's freedom?

"In related news, a confidential source has told our Capitol correspondent that freshman Congressman, Chris Edwards is working on another resolution that would counter H.R. 291. We will say more about that in a few minutes." The anchorman made it through the first segment of the thirty minute program. Although his broadcast was flawless, to those who were listening from the control room, something was missing.

Jessica James walked up to the open door in Congressman Edwards' office, where he was preparing to leave for the day. "Mr. Edwards?" he looked up from his work. "The evening news is on. You may want to see the next segment when the commercial break ends," she told him. He followed his assistant out into the main waiting area where a flat screened television was mounted to the wall just opposite of her desk. The news program had just come back on air, and he stood to listen quietly as Marvin Maddox began the next news segment.

"Just a few minutes ago, I reported to you of a new direction that Chris Edwards, a Constitution congressman from

South Carolina has taken," the anchorman was saying. "What seems to be an outward embracing of Christianity in his personal life has been interpreted by many to have influenced his political movements. And there are many who don't like it. Yesterday I interviewed Darrell Youngblood, the president of the National Association for Social Equality, for his views."

The screen flashed to another scene where both Marvin Maddox and Darrell Youngblood were sitting in opposite chairs. "Mr. Youngblood, what significance, if any, do you see in the opposition of the Constitution Party against the proposed H.R. 291?" the news anchor questioned the President of NASE. "For one, I think it's outright dangerous. When our legislators begin to endorse religion, that's the first step toward legislating their Christian beliefs." Youngblood responded. "Yes, but isn't Representative Jackson's bill that is hostile to Christianity reflect her own religious beliefs as well?" Maddox probed his interviewee. "Sara Jackson's bill is merely a safeguard against the religious bigotry that has taken over this nation," Darrell Youngblood countered defensively. "For too long we have been forced to listen to the claim that America was founded on a religion that is in fact, hostile to every person that doesn't hold to their biblical teachings." [20]

The screen returned to the live news program with Maddox announcing. "So there you have it; two opinions, in complete opposition to each other. Each one claiming that the other is a threat to the nation. This promises to be an interesting debate in the weeks to come. That's all for the UBC Evening News. Thank you all for joining us."

Congressman Edwards picked up the remote control and muted the channel. "Thank you for calling me," he told Jessica. "Let's follow this one closely." The congressman turned to pick up his planner before going home. He had already been cautioned that his stand would have strong opposition to his work. *"So this is how it feels,"* he thought to himself as he turned off the light and left the room.

7

Faith in Action

Saturday morning came all too early and found Congressman Edwards walking down the corridors of the Rayburn House Office Building to his office suite.   John Campbell, Amy Patterson, from Iowa, and Graham Gillespie, each of the Constitution Party were already sitting around the table. "Good morning, gentlemen; and Amy," he nodded to his colleagues.   Congressman Campbell started the meeting as he sat down. "We've been discussing some rather exciting topics I hope we can integrate into a draft bill to send to the floor." The senior congressman looked at Edwards. "I have been pleased to follow Chris' development of his own proposal," he continued. "I've made everyone a copy to see what is included on my draft," Edwards spoke up, passing copies of his outline around the table. They glanced at his proposal while Campbell continued talking. "Let's take both proposals a little further, and see if we can develop some ideas that our party can more readily be identified by." The others nodded in agreement. "And perhaps we can come up with something that will better unite us as a party. That is crucial to putting our own candidate back in the White House this fall."

The older congressman began handing out another packet of papers. Chris glanced over the coversheet of the packet he just received. *The Heritage and Freedom Amendments Act* was titled across the top of the page. Congressman Campbell gave everyone a few moments to read over the pamphlet. An outline of the proposed bill read:

To return the nation to economic security through:
1. Good economic policy: Congress shall pass an annual budget that does not exceed the total national revenue.
2. Elimination of the federal deficit: Congress shall reduce spending by one percent annually until the federal deficit has been removed. [CE-7]
3. Leadership accountability: Both houses of Congress shall exhibit good ethics and moral values through amending and implementing a new Congressional Code of Ethics:
   a. Enacting term limits for both Houses of Congress
   b. Mandating and enforcing disqualification from office for willful infraction of the Congressional Code of Ethics.
4. Restoring the integrity of the judicial system to its proper role to include:
   a. One 10 year term for appointments to the Supreme Court.
   b. Accountability within the Department of Justice.

Campbell seemed to have taken the lead role in the discussion, although this was not an official committee of the House. "Are there any specific questions or comments that anyone would like to address?" he invited the others' participation. "This is a good outline," Amy Patterson spoke up. "Except for the item on term limits. I'm surprised that you would endorse that one, since you've been in for so long." Campbell was thoughtful for a moment. "As long as this body can expect unlimited tenure, it will never get much accomplished. No one would want to return to their previous career with nothing to show for their time served in Congress. "As for me," he paused, "this bill, if passed, will be the single most important resolution I've ever worked on." The room was quiet for a few moments; they were touched that the senior congressman was willing to sponsor a bill that would take him out of office.

"We're headed in the right direction," Congressman Edwards spoke up. "But I think we need to go a step farther with some wording that specifically embraces the moral values that our nation's founders lived by." The committee members looked up, ready to hear his suggestions, but Congresswoman Patterson wasn't as receptive. "Let's not get too radical," she cautioned. "That change will come when we get the right man in office." Amy was in a tight race for re-election in the upcoming elections in November. Her state was equally split between Constitutional conservatives and Progressive Party members. With her office at stake, she was pressured to choose where she should stand in this matter.

The junior congressman leaned forward in his chair and lowered his voice. "An election won't fix what's wrong with America," he said firmly. "That's going to take a moral and spiritual awakening CE-8 and it can start right here." Ms. Patterson was taken aback for a moment, but quickly regained her position. "That may be," she countered, "But I can't support anything that could be interpreted as the State endorsing any Christian doctrine." But Edwards pressed his thoughts. "And I can't support a half-hearted bill that doesn't stand on specific moral standards. Our willful rejection of good morals is the root of this nation's problems."

The senior congressman raised his hand to calm the atmosphere down. "Let's save the debate for the floor," he encouraged them. They were all silent for a few moments; each one reflecting on the depth of the resolution's reach. The four lawmakers remained working through lunch to find a common ground with Congressman Edwards' last request. It was decided that Edwards and Campbell would fully develop their outlines into a written document that could be presented to the entire Congress.

Jordan walked through the kitchen door and laid a book on the table. He had spent the better part of the afternoon at the library working on his research paper. Connie stood next to the stove preparing the evening meal. The well-mannered teen sat down at the counter, wanting to talk. His mother turned around. "Has it been a rough day?" She asked when she saw the blank expression on his face. "It's been several," Jordan replied. She looked at him inquisitively. "Would you care to talk about it?" He hesitated again, and finally spoke. "It's Mrs. Crenshaw again." Jordan's mother dried her hands and sat down across from her son. "Several days ago, we had to turn in our topic for our research paper." He paused. "She turned mine down." "What was her reason?" Connie asked. "I wanted to do mine on how Christianity influenced early American history," he replied. "But she said that she couldn't allow anything that dealt with religion, even though she's teaching it in the classroom herself."

Connie was frustrated by another challenge to Jordan's beliefs in the same class; at the same time she was proud of her son's desire to use a religious theme for his report. "I was already working on the research. So what should I do?" he asked her quietly. "Well, you can either do your original topic, or ask her what she would prefer; but the decision is yours." Jordan had been hoping for an affirmation. "I've almost got it completed," he said, lighting back up. "Now, at least I don't have to start over!" Connie smiled at her son. "Everything will work out," she encouraged him. "I promise you."

Nancy was already at home when Chris walked through the door. She came into the living room to greet him. "How did it go today?" she asked. Ever since Chris shared his ideas about the resolution with her, the congressman's wife had taken a special interest in his work. Their jobs were demanding; both required an unusual amount of work compared to their previous life in Blue Ridge Heights. The two had committed to leave work at work in order to maintain a sense of family balance whenever they were home. But she wanted to follow its progress since Chris had developed such a passion for the resolution.

"This meeting was a confirmation that I'm on the right track. Several of my own ideas were exactly the same as the proposal the committee was already working on." He recounted the meeting to his wife. "That's wonderful!" Nancy congratulated her husband. He seemed to be in deep thought. "Is there something bothering you?" she asked. "Well," he sighed, "The others aren't ready to sign on to my thoughts about embracing our Judeo-Christian heritage." Nancy was thoughtful. "What are you asking for on that point?" she enquired. "I just think the amendments should allow Congress to measure its activity by the same standards our founding fathers lived by," he responded. "That won't mandate any Christian content, but it would allow their standards, which were shaped by their faith, to be considered.

Nancy felt her husband's frustration. "Don't give up," she encouraged him. "Your proposal has come a long way since you first started working on it. You won't get everyone's backing, but those that will stand behind it are the only ones that matter." Chris gazed into Nancy's eyes. He was blessed to have a wife who completely understood his thoughts and shared his passion for his work. Football practice would be over shortly, and the two sat down together to enjoy a few moments of solitude before the bustle began once Justin and Jamie came home.

Mrs. Crenshaw's class worked quietly on their study guides for the final exam. The students had turned their research papers in the day before. The teacher thumbed through a stack of reports as she waited for the afternoon bell to ring. She stopped shuffling through her students' assignments and looked more closely at Jordan's report. The cover-sheet read; *Early American History: A Christian Perspective.* The teacher picked up her pen and wrote something on it, and then carried it back to where Jordan sat and laid it on his desk. A large F circled in red was written on the cover page. Distracted by her movement, the students sitting near Jordan looked over to his desk. They were shocked at the grade she had assigned him without even reading the paper. Within moments the entire class was whispering excitedly. "Okay class," Mrs. Crenshaw spoke loudly to get their attention. You will be receiving your graded papers tomorrow." She paused a moment as her eyes met Jordan's. "Those who did not follow my instructions will receive a zero." An audible groan spread around the classroom as the bell rang.

Jordan threw his book bag over his shoulder and tried to get out of the class without talking with anyone. He was humiliated. "Jordan, wait up!" Emily rushed to catch up with him. Jordan turned as she spoke. They both stopped in the hall for a moment. "So, what are you going to do?" She asked. "I guess I'll just have to live with it," he shrugged his shoulders. "Or fight it," Emily prodded him. The entire class felt he had been wronged, and she was the mouthpiece. "I don't know," Jordan replied. "My dad's already done enough. I don't want to stir up any further controversy." He didn't know why his sister's best friend was suddenly so interested with the conflict between him and Mrs. Crenshaw. "Well, I think you should fight it," she replied, defensively. "Stupid teacher," she muttered as she walked away. Jordan smiled as he headed toward his next class. It was of some comfort that so many classmates were standing behind him.

Another week flew by for Congressman Edwards. He was encouraged by the progress of their new resolution. Jessica was already in the office and hard at work when he arrived on Friday morning. The congressman stopped in front of her desk. "If you would, make a call to the major news agencies," he requested. "Let them know that I'll be making an announcement downstairs at noon." Jessica wrote down his request so she would be prepared to make the calls as soon as business hours were open.

Senator Roger Francis stepped out of the Senate Conference Room after a long overdue meeting with several of the Progressive Party's key senators. These were the ones to whom he was entrusting his presidential future. Each one had made a commitment to promote a different aspect of the efforts to have him elected as the next President of the United States. As he got off the elevator he nearly ran into Thomas Wainwright, who was passing by. The two walked to Francis' office together. Senator Francis had a tight schedule for the rest of the day, but he had become accustomed to the continual interruptions that his campaign brought with it. They settled in two Queen Anne chairs in the corner of his office. The well-known publicist was curious as to the nature of his request to meet, because they were already scheduled to meet tomorrow.

"I called," the senator said, "because of a new piece of legislation that could be a serious threat to our campaign." Wainwright raised his eyebrows. "Really?" he spoke up. "Fill me in." The senator's publicist settled in to listen. "Representative Sara Jackson, from Nevada has submitted H.R. 291," Senator Francis explained to his publicist. Wainwright was already familiar with the bill, but continued listening. "This resolution will call for more stringent measures to the nation's hate crime laws. It even provides for severe penalties for both pastors and Church members, who openly criticize any individual who is in a protected social class." The publicist stopped writing and asked, "How would this affect you?" he asked. "If this even gets to the floor I'm sure I'll be asked my opinion in the opening presidential debate."

Mr. Wainwright took a deep breath. "You can either disconnect yourself from your party's stand altogether, or create a diversion to take attention away from the bill until it has been passed." The publicist sat back with a smile. He could spin any negative scenario in a way that would turn it into an asset for his client. "Yes, but how do you propose?" Senator Francis wasn't clear on what Wainwright was suggesting. "You can start with that young congressman that's been in the news lately...what's his name? Congressman Edwards, from South Carolina," Thomas almost lost his train of thought. "Try to dig up anything about him you can find. It's my understanding he's working on an ethics reform proposal. Find something on him, and it's sure to cause a stir."

Senator Francis was surprised. "Where did you learn that? It's the first I've heard anything from his end of the House." "That's why you hired me," the publicist said almost arrogantly, standing to leave. "I'm sorry to rush out, but I have an appointment in an hour. Don't say anything in public about this subject until we meet tomorrow. I'll come up with the best way to address it." He strode quickly toward the door, but stopped and turned around. "Don't forget the old standby," he told the senator. "If you suggest the opposition is a hate-monger, you've planted the seed, and he has no defense." He turned toward the door again and left the office. Senator Francis was thoughtful. He hadn't considered this, but maybe it would work. The senator hesitated a moment before picking up the telephone.

It was lunch hour in the Rayburn House Office Building. The halls were full of congressmen and their staff members walking toward the cafeteria. Congressman Edwards headed down the main corridor leading to the large entrance area. As he approached the foyer several television cameras had already been set up near the center of the room. Marvin Maddox spotted the congressman approaching and stood up to greet him when he walked up. His news director had requested him to do this interview at the last minute. The anchorman rarely worked "in the field," since taking the anchor's chair, but enjoyed a change of pace from the rigid structure of the studio.

Edwards recognized the anchorman from his evening news reports on the UBC channel. He extended his hand to greet the television journalist. "Good afternoon, Mr. Maddox. I'm Chris Edwards," he introduced himself merely out of formality. After exchanging greetings, Edwards spoke with him for a few minutes while the television crew finished getting their gear prepared. He had a good feeling about the reporter, yet sensed that he might have felt ill at ease for some reason. *"Perhaps he's never interviewed a congressman before?"* he thought to himself.

A crewmember signaled that they were ready, and the two men went to the spot marked in front of the camera. The cameraman motioned with his fingers, "Three, two, one..." he pointed toward the two men, indicating that the camera was recording.

"Today we bring to you an interesting development from the Capitol, in the Rayburn House Office Building where a large number of our lawmakers go to work each day," Marvin Maddox announced, facing the camera. "In direct contrast to the recently announced House Resolution sponsored by Sara Jackson, a new grassroots effort has been started by a number of other congressmen. The goal of their coalition is to present a resolution that would effectively destroy the congresswoman's bill. South Carolina Congressman Chris Edwards is here to explain its contents." the reporter turned to face the congressman. "Congressman Edwards, can you give us an overview of the proposed resolution you've been working on?" he questioned.

"Thank you, Marvin," Edwards responded to his interviewer. "The goal of this proposal, which we have designated as the *Heritage and Freedom Amendments Act*, is to reaffirm some of our founders' ideals and return the country to a sense of proper balance." He paused for a short breath. "Are you able to get into more of the specifics of this bill?" the reporter continued his interview. "Well, in order to engage the American public in our efforts for national change, it must first start with its leadership," Chris Edwards had transitioned comfortably into his interview. "Our nation is disenfranchised by Congress. A great part of our resolution calls for radical change from the White House, to Congress, and even the Supreme Court, including term limits on Congress and the Court. This will actually require amendments to the Constitution. It will embrace several other specifics dealing with budget concerns, and even a possible resolution that would affirm our Judeo-Christian values."

Maddox turned back to face the camera. "These measures, together with House Resolution 291, promise to give

100

us an interesting show in the weeks and months ahead. Thank you, congressman, for being with us today." The anchorman and congressman both stood still until the operator gave them the signal that they were off the air, and then turned to shake hands.

"Thank you for your interview," Marvin spoke graciously to the congressman. "Thank you for your interest in our work," Chris responded. "Perhaps we will have the opportunity to sit down off the record someday?" Marvin was touched by the congressman's kind gesture. "It would be my honor to do so," he said graciously. They spoke for a few more minutes before Congressman Edwards excused himself. Despite his progress, as he returned to his office he still had a nagging feeling that he should go even further in pressing for his resolution; and that would come with a price.

Darkness enveloped the U.S. Capitol as congressmen began pulling in the parking lot to start another day. Menacing clouds hovered over the historic district, foretelling an approaching storm. Congressman Edwards couldn't help but think that perhaps another storm, a political one, was on the horizon as he made his way down the freeway. Inside the Rayburn House Office Building, Sara Jackson hurried down the long corridor, hoping to catch several colleagues before they reached their offices. Progressive Party Congressman James Callahan, from California was just leaving his office suite for a meeting. He turned to face Jackson when he heard her footsteps approaching. "I'm so glad I caught up with you," she greeted him. She wasn't planning to go into detail, but merely wanted to ask for her colleague's consideration for more support on her bill. "It will only take a moment," she persuaded him. "I have a minute," he replied.

"Things have gotten a little more complicated since Edwards made his announcement," she told her colleague. "I do appreciate your support, but I need to be sure you'll be willing to stand by it, if things should get out of hand." They stepped out of the way to allow several other congressmen walking down the hallway to pass by. "When I sign on a bill, I'm there for the duration," Callahan assured her. "But have you gotten any other support?" "We have several who are considering," she said. "But perhaps the most notable one is Amy Patterson." Callahan raised his eyebrows. This was interesting. "Keep working on her," he encouraged her. "There's a reason why she's not totally committed to the Edwards bill." If they could convince her to support H.R. 291, she might convince several of her own constituents. Before parting, the two agreed to meet with any new supporters for an informal discussion on Jackson's resolution the next week.

After reaching his office, Congressman Edwards leaned back in his office chair and closed his eyes to relax for a few moments. Life had taken some interesting turns over the one year he had been in public office. It wasn't that long ago that he had become disillusioned by all the corruption and indifference that surrounded him. He had almost lost interest in his work. Then he got up, began talking to others who had influenced him, about his feelings. He did something about it. After a mere several weeks of struggling to make sense out of his purpose and trying to regain his passion, the thought suddenly occurred to him that now, he was doing what he had once thought was impossible. Others were listening to him. People of influence had noticed his passion, and what's more, were supporting his efforts. Some were dug in like a stubborn mule against his ideas of change, but his camp was growing larger. Edwards sat up in his chair and began scrolling through the contact list on his cell phone. He stopped at Scott Crawford's name, and hit the call button.

Pastor Scott was in such deep thought as he was returning from visiting an elderly Church member in the hospital that he missed the driveway of the Church parking lot. He was jolted back to reality by the vibration of his cell phone in his shirt pocket. He put the phone to his ear. "This is Pastor Scott," he answered. "Good afternoon, Scott," the congressman greeted him from the other end. The young pastor turned around and pulled back into the Church parking lot. "I've hesitated to call you over the past several weeks because the progress has been so slow," Edwards could hardly wait to get it out. He didn't have long to talk but would take the time necessary to bring his spiritual adviser abreast of the latest developments they both had been hoping for.

"Do you remember me telling you about the new bill by Sara Jackson?" he prodded the pastor's memory. "I believe she's from Nevada?" the pastor asked. "Yes," the congressman was beginning to articulate his thoughts more clearly. "You may remember the federal hate crime law that was enacted back in 2009?" [21] Scott remembered the passing of this law vividly. It was passed in response to the brutal murder of a college student by a gang because they believed he was gay. Another crime related to the law was of a heinous murder by two white supremacists who dragged a black man behind a truck. "Her bill would impose some severe penalties for both pastors and Church members, who openly criticize individuals based on their biblical beliefs. In short, the bill is so nebulous that anyone could potentially be prosecuted for merely offending someone's

103

personal beliefs, he told the pastor. The problem with this if it passes, is, how far will they go after that?"

Scott was disturbed. With open criticism of the Church's beliefs and teaching becoming stronger by the day, he thought that he had heard it all. But this proposed legislation was most concerning. "How can this bill even be considered, since free speech is constitutionally protected? I mean, where does it stop?" he posed to his congressman? "That's the thing," Edwards continued. "Legally it can't be done, but if we continue to sit back and allow just a few to present such radical propositions, it could very well slip through the back door, and lead to the first amendment being destroyed."

Edwards remembered the main purpose of his call. "That's the reason I was calling you," he continued. "In some ways, I feel that we're making progress on the Heritage and Freedom bill, but Sara's resolution could destroy its chances. We need your prayers." His request sounded like a passionate plea, and the pastor assured him that not only would he do so, but he would also call his congregation to a time of special prayer for God's direction on the Congress as they began the debate.

8

Spiritual Warfare

On his way back to the studio, Marvin Maddox wondered why he had been asked to do a field interview with Congressman Edwards. He had performed other interviews at the Capitol, but this was the first major piece of legislation he had covered that would involve follow up reporting. Now, back at his office, Harold Gentry knocked on his door and entered the room.

"How did it go?" his news director inquired. "Without a hitch," the anchorman responded, still feeling positive about his interview with the lawmaker. "The congressman was passionate about the resolution. He gave a clear and concise statement that the people will find easy to understand." Maddox's superior cleared his throat. "Well, I want you to undo all of that," he instructed the anchorman. "I'm not sure I understand?" Marvin was confused. "Something we have to understand as news journalists is that we don't merely report events. A greater part of our work is in shaping these events." Maddox still didn't seem to understand what he was saying, so the news director continued. "Your job is to convey more than just the facts. We must report it in the best way that is for the good of the country."

Marvin remained silent, trying to process what he had just been told. "Listen," Harold persisted. "These Constitution politicians are focused on forcing their radical propaganda and religious beliefs on the rest of the country. Our job is to balance their perspective. In a greater sense, we are social engineers." He stopped so his words could sink in. "Just keep that in mind." The news director stood and left the room. Marvin was stunned. Not report the mere facts? Did that mean he was supposed to shape the public's opinion by what he-or rather, the network wanted them to know? As an entry level reporter he had never dealt with such an issue. But he was feeling increasing pressure to steer away from the facts of many current events ever since being promoted to the anchor's chair. It went against his personal journalistic philosophy; it went against his personal morals. For the rest of the afternoon, Marvin could hardly focus on his preparation for the evening broadcast.

The remainder of the week, as well as the weekend flew by quickly for Congressman Edwards. He had planned for a few days of rest in anticipation for the upcoming week, but due to both the pending Jackson Bill and the *Heritage and Freedom Amendments Act* he was co-sponsoring, there was much work to be accomplished. He spent the majority of the weekend working on some final thoughts to be used in his debate. Monday morning came all too quickly for the congressman, and he arrived at the office a little earlier than usual. A Supreme Court Ruling on the *Church vs. San Esteban, CA case* had been anticipated, and the lawmakers were sure that Monday was the day it would be handed down. Although rulings from the high court generally weren't posted until later in the afternoon, Edwards needed to get several pending items completed as early as possible. He wanted to spend the rest of the day reviewing the ruling, and maybe even discuss it further with his colleagues if in fact it was handed down.

Congressman Edwards' office was unusually quiet throughout the entire morning. So quiet, that he didn't notice that his office staff had left for lunch. He was interrupted by the sound of the door in the front office opening as he diligently worked on his resolution. The congressman looked up as Jessica walked in the office with a folder in her hands. "I think you've been waiting for this," she said to Chris as she handed him the folder. Edwards thanked his assistant as he opened it and glanced at the page on the inside. "U.S. Supreme Court, *Church v. San Esteban, CA,*" was printed at the top of the page. The congressman hastily continued reading.

> *"In the case of the Church v. San Esteban, the court will postpone its ruling to allow more time for further consideration of all relevant issues."*

"Unusual," he thought. For the next several minutes, Chris reviewed the facts regarding the case to himself. After all, the outcome could have a critical effect on his resolution.

Steve Williams drove by the Church before returning to the school for the rest of the day. He closed the door and walked around the corner to speak with Pastor Crawford. Another teacher had just alerted him that the students were talking about Mrs. Crenshaw's latest run-in with Jordan. He wanted to stay in communication with his pastor, since it involved his son. Scott looked up from his work when he heard his youth pastor come in. "I'm afraid there's more bad news," Steve said after greeting his pastor. "As the principal, I try to avoid conflict if at all possible. But as his youth pastor, I'm proud of Jordan for standing up for his faith." Scott nodded in agreement. "That's what we've tried to teach both Jordan and Brianna to do. But sometimes there are consequences for doing the right thing." Steve paused a moment before his reply. "I think you should take it to the next level," he told the pastor. "We've discussed this issue several times before. My hands are tied from an educators' position, so the school board is the next step." Both men agreed to keep each other informed of any developments from each others' end. After telling Connie that he was leaving, Scott followed his youth pastor out the door and drove to the school district office.

Dr. David Gambrell walked out of the campus chapel and strolled down the sidewalk to where his car was parked on the side of the street. He liked to think of the chapel as the tabernacle in the Old Testament. It was located at the center of the campus, symbolic of strong spiritual emphasis placed in the daily life of its students. Whether the students were enrolled in a secular course of study or a Bible or ministry major, the entire student body was required to attend the weekly chapel service. Dr. Gambrell presented the message each week, but on occasion, invited a special speaker to address the student body in his place.

The president drove across the campus to return to his office. He would not be staying long, so he parked in front of the administration building instead of his usual parking space at the side entrance. As he walked toward his office, he was startled by a young man who had just stood up in the waiting area and was standing directly in his path. Marcus Jefferson extended his hand with an arrogant smile. Dr. Gambrell shook the young man's hand and prepared for what might come next. "Good afternoon, Marcus," he said congenially, while trying not to show that he had been taken off guard. The smile on the alumnus' face turned to a serious expression. "I'll get right to the point," he responded. "I'm here to notify you that I have petitioned the National Association for Social Equality. We are filing a formal complaint to the Department of Justice against King University for civil rights violations." The former student was intending to shake his former Bible Professor. But Dr. Gambrell had been preparing for this moment after receiving his previous letter from the former student. Still, he didn't know how far he would take it. His personal visit was unnecessary, considering that the college would be served an official notice of the complaint. His motive was clear; to simply rub the issue in deeper.

"What do you base your complaints on?" Dr. Gambrell inquired. "We allege that students' civil rights have been violated by not allowing them to openly express their personal sexual preferences." Dr. Gambrell looked at Marcus sharply. "Young man," he responded assertively. "No rights have been violated on this campus. All students must agree to abide by our scriptural beliefs before being accepted. Because of the very nature of this school, we do not accept students who have not expressed a personal testimony as a Christian believer. Whether it is adultery, LGBT, or any other religious beliefs, any lifestyle not in harmony with the Bible is unacceptable for students on this campus."

Marcus' subtle smirk returned. "That's where you err," he replied. The law requires all non-profit institutions to have a non-discrimination policy for their employees and students." He was sure he had scored the final point on this one. "While you may be partially correct, the courts have consistently upheld religious institutions to discriminate, when it concerns issues that violate their religious convictions," the president countered. [22] "Well, consider yourself served," the young man turned and left without another word.

Dr. Gambrell opened the door to his office, where he retreated to his desk to get his mind off the confrontation. For years the large institution had been fought by outsiders because of their strong stand for fundamental doctrines of the Bible. Although they did not embrace any philosophy that was considered legalistic, they faithfully adhered to their convictions. The president of the university realized this would more than likely be an extended struggle, and began to mentally prepare for a drawn out battle.

Darrell Youngblood, President of the National Association for Social Equality, sat at a desk in his office at the organization's national headquarters. NASE was an advocacy organization whose mission was advancing the rights of individuals who were classified as the "alternative lifestyle community." While the national statistics for the gay and lesbian population was an extreme minority, [23] their mission was to promote their cause and give them a larger platform through their widespread activism.

Already, this organization was responsible for changing the political platforms in over ten states. Those running for public office across the nation took note of their activity, and were slowly changing their approach to the alternative living community in order to retain their vote. Forty-five states had legalized same-sex marriage, and the goal was to permeate the entire society and have this union legalized in all 50 states.[CE-3] A Supreme Court ruling on this issue was expected to be handed down in less than six months, and they were certain it would swing in their favor. The efforts of NASE were largely successful due to the Church's, and conservative political constituency's unwillingness to present a united opposition to their agenda. Many communities that were considered as committed to Judeo-Christian conservative values simply had not taken their activism seriously; this gave the organization a larger voice in the national community. These issues were becoming a major source of contention between the Constitution and Progressive Parties, and even threatened to fragment the Constitution Party within its own constituency.

The telephone on Darrell's desk rang, and he paused from his work to answer. "National Association for Social Equality," he answered. It was Marcus Jefferson. "Do you have a minute?" he asked the officer of the organization. "I'm open. What's the latest?" Darrell asked. "I just spoke with Dr. Gambrell in person," Marcus reported. The two activists had met earlier that week. Darrell had become interested in the school only a few months earlier when he was contacted by Marcus. NASE was always looking for an open door for new avenues to challenge, and Marcus had given them a good opportunity to establish their activism in the Charlotte area.

To date, the association had focused on state and federal agencies in trying to influence public policy against Christian values. They had recently fought a vicious battle against a nationally known department store to try to force them to change the businesses' policy of operating by its owner's Christian beliefs. Now, it was time to launch an all out attack against Christian schools. If they were successful in this campaign, the entire country would see a total collapse of the Judeo-Christian conservative values that NASE claimed as bigoted and discriminating against society.

"What's the next step?" Marcus asked the activist. "After the public has been conditioned to our presence, there will be much less resistance when we file for action against the school," Darrell responded. "But if we move too quickly, there will be a strong outcry from Christian supporters." Marcus was pleased in playing a part to hopefully, bring some harm to the school he had fought against for so long. "When we meet with the legal team," Youngblood continued, "our attorney will ask you everything you know that applies to the discrimination suit. You must be familiar with anything you could possibly be asked about the school." Marcus was agreeable with the plan; but then, he heard a quiet voice speaking to him, *"This is wrong."* After completing their conversation and hanging up, the young man returned to his motel room disturbed by a new voice, now speaking to him.

The congressmen began filing in the House Chamber before the morning session began. The two hot issues, H.R. 291, and the *Heritage and Freedom Amendments Act*, were expected to be addressed today, but had been postponed until later in the month. Today, the discussion would be focused on yet another attempt to pass a national balanced budget.

Over the past seven years, the House of Representatives had sent numerous proposed budgets to the Senate, but each one was repeatedly shot down. During this time the national deficit had rocketed from 10 trillion to 25 trillion dollars. Congressman Edwards couldn't understand why Congress continued to discount the seriousness of the situation. To Edwards, those who were standing in the way were being restrained by some invisible force.

All the while, the citizen's perception was that Congress had turned a deaf ear to public screams to stop the out of control government spending. And they were right. Congress continued passing temporary measures to keep the country going, but still turning a blind eye to the ever increasing national debt. To some, it was like chess; a game of strategy whose winner would cripple the other party. To compound the nation's financial woes, the national unemployment rate had risen to 14%. Many had simply given up on finding a job and were turning to welfare for their support. In fact, well over sixty million Americans were now on some sort of public support-a figure that was totally unsustainable. This, coupled with the national deficit, threatened an imminent economic collapse.

Congressman Edwards sat at his desk wondering if today's outcome would be any different. He and a growing number of congressmen were fed-up by the gridlock that controlled the Capitol. *"If a house is divided against itself, that house cannot stand."* [24] These words of Jesus rang in his ears. *"But how can this division be broken?"* Edwards wondered, as he waited for the morning roll call.

Inside the White House, the Cabinet Room next to the Oval Office began filling with the President's cabinet members. This executive conference room faced the Rose Garden, and was elaborately decorated with long curtains, chandeliers and leather chairs. The President was always punctual for his meetings, but just as he was preparing to leave, his executive assistant entered the office to announce the arrival of Aaron Crosby, his national security adviser. President Duncan stood to greet his adviser, and invited him to have a seat.

"Thank you, Mr. President," the adviser greeted President Duncan as he sat down. Aaron got right to the purpose for his meeting. "Our intelligence indicates an increase in the conflict between Israel and Hamas over the past several weeks," he informed the Commander-in-Chief. "The IDF has instructed their fighter jets to be ready for an imminent strike against targets in Gaza." The President raised his eyebrows. In spite of repeated attacks against Israel by their arch enemy, they had been unusually quiet for several years. During this time their Prime

Minister had not communicated with the U.S. State Department as often as he had in the past. The last time he spoke with the Secretary of State, he had been alerted that they were drawing a red line, and would launch an all out attack if provoked any further.

Israel contended that Palestine was the actual location of the ancient land of Israel. Their claim was based on the *Torah*, [25] or the first five books of the *Tanakh,* the Jewish sacred scriptures; also in the Old Testament of the Holy Bible. It included an account of God giving the land to Abraham, the father of the Jewish nation. [26] To the contrary, Palestinian Arabs asserted that their continuous majority status as residents of the territory gave them the right to control it. Since Jews and Christians both shared the common belief that the Law of Moses was divinely inspired, both held to Israel's rightful claim to all of the land. And they were hated throughout the Middle East. [27]

The President understood the seriousness of the dilemma. Regardless of the Jewish Nation's past concessions for the sake of peace, [28] if they retaliated, it could launch an all out blood bath in the region. Israel had already expressed that they would not tolerate any further threat from Iran, who had openly threatened to "wipe them off the map." [29] Now they were vowing to defend their territory, with or without outside help. With the United States' military presence in the Middle East, the possibility of another long term engagement on foreign soil was still likely. *"But if Israel becomes involved..."* President Duncan thought quietly. "Let me know if there's the slightest move toward an attack." The Commander in Chief thanked Aaron for his briefing. Due to this sudden turn of events, He would have to cut the cabinet meeting short so he could meet with his joint chiefs of staff.

The call for adjournment in the House Chamber was made, and the lawmakers began leaving the chamber. Aside from their effort to again submit a budget proposal that the Senate would agree on, another refreshing resolution had been submitted to the floor and passed unanimously. Over the past several years, an increasing awareness of Christians being persecuted in other countries had been made. Religious persecution had been going on for years, but it wasn't until the onset of social media, that it had become more widely known to the general public. Just last month, a Christian pastor in a mid-eastern country was executed for refusing to deny his Christian faith. And the public had become aware of another senseless massacre of an entire Church, including women and children who refused to deny their faith in Jesus Christ. Another radical terrorist organization had slaughtered thousands of Christians in several mid-eastern countries. Such instances of Christians being persecuted had become a near-daily occurrence. And no one seemed to care. *"How long will it be before we see Christians in America lose their lives for the faith?"* Edwards wondered. Today the House of Representatives sent a direct letter to the President asking him to intervene on yet another pending execution in the same country if this pastor didn't deny his faith. It was refreshing to see that this petition passed unanimously, especially involving a matter of such importance. *"It is possible to work together after all, even in critical matters,"* Edwards thought as he returned to his office. The congressman was anxious to get his weekly briefing from Jessica. He had missed the morning meeting with his assistant, and wanted to address all important issues before leaving for the day.

Sunday attendance at the Trinity Christian Fellowship was up over the past several months. This, coupled with his involvement as a spiritual counselor to their congressman, had given Pastor Crawford a renewed sense of purpose. He remained optimistic that the community would become more united, and some good could come from the controversy involving Jordan's History class.

This morning he approached the pulpit with an unusual sense of urgency. He felt that his congregation's stand should not just be a local one; it could also have an influence on the national level. "Over the last several months, our community has experienced an attack that many have perceived as personal," the pastor introduced his message. "To some, the issue may appear trite. But all over America, our Christian values have come under more and more attacks, almost by the day," he continued. "Right now, a bill is being debated in Washington that could affect our very own religious freedoms-not in another country, but in a land that was established so that Christian liberties could be forever spread. This morning I will be speaking to you on the topic of "Spiritual Warfare," because this is not merely a physical battle. It is a battle for the very heart and soul of all men."

Wesley and Karen Crenshaw, who sat on the second row, were both uncomfortable as they listened to their pastor speak. They had become increasingly dissatisfied with the sudden sense of conscience spreading around the community. Karen's once comfortable job as a history teacher had been challenged by several Church members; people who were supposed to be her friends. She couldn't understand why they had made such a big deal about just one lesson in particular. And the pastor's preaching had changed noticeably over the last several months. *"He's already meddled in the classroom,"* Wesley thought to himself. *"Now he's bringing politics into the pulpit."* But an inward voice was calling Wesley to surrender, although he didn't realize who was speaking.

116

During the lunch hour on Monday, a breaking news flash came across the flat screened TVs mounted throughout the House Office Building Cafeteria. It turned the attention of lawmakers and staff members to the announcement, about to take place. A picture of the White House came across the screen, and then switched to the Oval Office where the President sat behind his desk.

"Good afternoon," President Duncan began speaking. "My national security team has alerted me of an imminent confrontation between Israel and the Palestinians that could exceed any previous attack in several decades. While the United States recognizes Israel as a sovereign nation, they are only one, among many in that territory," he paused. "Due to the tension between the Jews and Palestinians, their actions could be detrimental to the overall peace of the entire region. Given the seriousness of such a conflict and the length of time it would take Congress to draft a resolution, I will ask the United Nations Security Council to recommend sanctions against Israel if they retaliate."

A buzz of excited talk spread around the cafeteria. Congressmen from both parties were disturbed by the President's announcement. How could he lay the blame of disrupting peace on Israel when surrounding nations were threatening *their own* security? This was by far, the most provocative directive the President had ever proposed, especially since it involved the United States' main ally in the Middle East. Many of the lawmakers finished their lunches prematurely and stood to move back to their offices. This news was certain to commence a nationwide call-in to their offices from concerned citizens.

Aaron Crosby sat quietly at his table over in the corner. He was anguished that the president had rejected his advice. *"If we turn against Israel,"* he thought, *"how will this affect our own nation's safety?"*

The mail truck pulled into the Church parking lot and carried a large bundle of mail into the office. Scott had just arrived back at the office after visiting a sick Church member. He greeted the mail carrier at the door. "Good afternoon, pastor," the postman responded as he handed the stack of mail to Scott. "You have a good day." He smiled and returned to his jeep. The pastor thumbed through the stack of mail and stopped when he saw an envelope with "School District of Appalachian County" printed across its top. The pastor laid the rest of the stack down, opened the envelope and began reading.

> Dear Rev. Crawford,
> We are writing to notify you of the school
> board's decision regarding your son's
> classroom instruction and assignments. The
> board has unanimously agreed that your child's
> rights were not violated. We appreciate
> your inquiry; however, our policy will remain
> the same.
> Sincerely,
> Kenneth Wiley,
> Superintendent

The pastor laid the letter on his desk. He had hoped that voicing his concerns would correct what he believed was religious indoctrination in the school, however isolated it might have been. Since the school was firm in their resolve to allow this instruction to the exclusion of any Christian beliefs, maybe he should appeal this decision?

The small group of congressmen working together had grown to a regular weekly meeting, as each one worked on a separate section of the proposed legislation. Today they were gathered in the executive lounge of the Rayburn Office Building. This resolution was far different from the typical bills that so often, benefited no none other than the Washington establishment itself. The *Heritage and Freedom Amendments Act* would begin with a radical reform of all three branches of the federal government; but Congressman Edwards still wanted more definite language that acknowledged the nation's traditional morals. But he conceded with the others to work with them to get this initial bill passed. If national leaders would order their work by good ethical standards, it would naturally lead to a greater awareness of how the nation's past virtues helped it to prosper.

The House Speaker had just sat down with them when Chaplain Peter Cartwright walked into the room. "Good afternoon, gentlemen," the chaplain greeted them cordially. Cartwright was well-respected among the lawmakers, and they always welcomed his presence. "Pull up a chair," John Campbell gestured with his open arm, and then shook his hand.

The chaplain dragged a chair from an empty table several feet away and sat down across from Congressman Edwards. In addition to the formal role he played as their spiritual counselor and representative at official functions, it was customary for the chaplain to associate with the lawmakers as the occasion arose. After some brief chatter, he leaned forward, preparing to change the subject. "I would like to invite each of you to join me for a morning prayer in the chapel," he proposed. "Don't you already have a weekly Bible study?" Congressman Wilson enquired. "I do," the chaplain responded. "But given the present state of affairs in America, I want to devote specific time to intercede for Divine intervention for our nation." Everyone at the table agreed that America *was* in a state of decline, and perhaps, even headed for an unprecedented crisis. But no one spoke up, except Congressman Edwards. "I'll be there," he promised the chaplain. There was an awkward silence as the other congressmen quietly left the table with no further promises of support for the chaplain's request.

The telephone rang on Harold Gentry's desk in the newsroom at the UBC Studio. He stopped his typing momentarily to answer it. "Newsroom, this is Harry," he said. Jessica James took a deep breath on the other end of the line. "May I speak with the news director?" she asked. "This is he. How can I help you?" the news executive responded. "My name is Jessica James. I'm Congressman Chris Edwards' executive assistant," she continued. Gentry grabbed a pen and began scribbling hastily on a piece of paper. "I'm calling because I'm being harassed by the congressman." Harold interrupted her. "Ma'am, if you're interested in blowing the whistle, I can help you," he told his caller. "But I need a written statement before we can air what you're telling me. When can we meet?" he asked Jessica. I'll be leaving early today," she replied. "Can you come to the War House Café at two o'clock?" The news director agreed to meet and then hung up the phone. He left his office, after telling his secretary that he would be back that afternoon.

Several blocks away from the House Office Building, Senator Francis' office was abuzz with activity in the Russell Senate Office Building. With the final debate approaching, the senator had delegated all but the most pressing matters to Reid Davis, his executive assistant. Although the senator had been in a meeting with his campaign manager for most of the day, his staff worked diligently to carry out their regular duties coupled with the additional load brought on by his presidential campaign. The telephone rang, and Reid picked up the receiver. "Senator Francis' Office, this is Reid Davis speaking," he answered. It was Jessica James. "If you could leave a message with the senator, I'd appreciate it," she requested. "Please tell him that the package he was sending to our office hasn't arrived." "I'll do so as soon as he returns," he replied to her request. The assistant hung up the phone, inwardly troubled by a feeling that something just wasn't right.

9

A Deluge of Distress

Students poured out of classes across the campus of King University. It was nearing the end of the school term. Both students and faculty alike were preparing for final exams. In the library, they rushed to complete their research papers and take care of last minute assignments. Not far away, professors were busy grading a flood of final assignments. Upstairs in the administration building, Dr. Gambrell was handling another crisis that could not have come at a more inopportune time. His administrative assistant walked through the open door in his office and handed him a letter she had already screened. *"U.S. District Court, Charlotte, NC,"* was centered at the top of the letterhead she handed him. It was addressed to the attention of Dr. David Gambrell. The president of the university sat down behind his desk and began reading:

Dear Dr. Gambrell and Directors,
You are hereby notified that the National Association
for Social Equality has filed a lawsuit against
King University for civil rights violations. You
shall appear for a preliminary hearing at the U.S.
District Court, in Charlotte, NC on Monday,
May 20, at 9:00 AM.
Yours very truly,
Samuel Barrington,
Clerk of Court

The telephone rang just as Dr. Gambrell completed reading the letter. He picked up the receiver to answer the call. "David Gambrell speaking," he answered. It was Jesse Wood, the chairman of the school's board of directors. "Good morning, David. I just received a legal notice in the mail. Have you received anything?" the director asked Dr. Gambrell. "I'm reading it right now," Gambrell responded. The school's president was glad the chairman had called. He would need to stay in close communication with the board as he prepared to respond to the legal action. "I'll contact the other directors today. Let me know as soon as you get an idea where this is going to go." Dr. Gambrell laid the telephone back in its cradle and prepared to re-schedule his day. He could only pray that it would be a short-lived effort, but he knew that a difficult battle lay ahead.

These fears were confirmed a few moments later when his phone rang again. "Its campus police," his administrative assistant announced, and then transferred the call to him. The director of campus security informed the school president that a group of protesters were gathering on the sidewalk near the front of the campus. The university campus was bordered with an elaborate wrought iron fence, and the main entrance had a security office with two guards on duty to monitor incoming traffic at all times. Fortunately, the protestors had not tried to enter, but Dr. Gambrell instructed his security director to notify the police department to request their presence. He hung the phone up again and returned to his work, hoping there wouldn't be any more bad news.

Members of the House of Representatives sat down after the opening invocation by Chaplain Cartwright. A.J. Wilson motioned for him to remain standing as he approached the podium to address the Congress. "Before we begin the morning session," the Speaker of the House began, "I recently spoke with our chaplain, who has expressed his desire to begin a daily early morning prayer on behalf of our country. I would like to offer the floor to him so he can share his thoughts with you personally."

A hushed whisper echoed around the room. Congresswoman Jackson stood up and interrupted before the chaplain could begin speaking. "For the record, I object to this presentation," she spoke out loudly. "Chaplain Cartwright has my highest respect, but he has no business speaking to this assembly outside of his stated responsibilities." Congressman Wilson stepped back to the microphone. "With all due respect, we have, on occasion extended the courtesy to unique individuals to address this body, and as the Speaker of the House, it is my privilege to invite such speakers," he countered.

"Mr. Speaker, you have openly endorsed the influence of one religion over this Congress-in fact, our entire country, and that is unlawful," the congresswoman protested. Congressman Wilson cleared his throat. "Ms. Jackson, it is my understanding that you personally contend that there is no God. If that is so," the House Speaker paused for a moment, "then a morning prayer won't influence anything," he said, trying to suppress a smile. A ripple of laughter circled the room, and Sara Jackson sat down without a further word. Chris was thankful that the Speaker had stood up for the chaplain. Congressman Wilson turned to address Chaplain Cartwright. "Chaplain, you are commended you for your dedication to this Congress and our country. I look forward to joining you tomorrow morning." All but Congresswoman Sara Jackson and a few of her close constituents rose to their feet in a concert of applause.

The hallways of the Blue Ridge Heights Academy had gone from the constant sound of teachers instructing their students, to the buzz of teens talking, restless for the end of the school term to arrive. Steve Williams passed by stacks of textbooks waiting to be returned to the book room. Kenneth Wiley, the School District Superintendent had just entered the building as the principal was walking into the front lobby. "Good day, Ken," he greeted the superintendent. The two men walked into the front office together. Mr. Wiley handed Steve a small book. "More controversy," the superintendent responded as he passed the book to Steve. He had dreaded meeting with his principal ever since the board's decision to uphold Mrs. Crenshaw's grade given to Jordan Crawford. "A group called, 'Citizens against Bible Bigotry,' has petitioned the court for permission to distribute this trash." Steve glanced at it and read the title; "*A Perverted Religion.*" In smaller words below the title were written: "*The whole truth about the whole Bible.*" He handed the booklet back to his superintendent. "Not on my watch," he said emphatically. Mr. Wiley hung his head. "They've sued for equal access to the schools," he said quietly. "The judge ruled in their favor since Bibles are distributed to students each year." CE-9

126

Steve was quiet for a moment as he took the booklet back and thumbed through it. Its introduction labeled Jesus as a pedophile. "We can fight it," Steve spoke up. "I'm sorry, but the board voted not to appeal. The legal fees would drain our budget." Steve was frustrated. The principal knew his superintendent was against the book being brought in, but wasn't one for confrontation. He, on the other hand wouldn't hesitate to stand up for principle, even though it had gotten him in trouble once or twice in the past. He would bring this to the attention of his pastor, and Kelly Graham. As soon as the Superintendent had left, Steve went back into his office to call the PTA president.

Several days of tension at King University had finally come to an end. What was expected to be a short-lived protest by NASE had turned into a three-day event, with demonstrators gathering each day before sun-up, carrying signs and chanting, "Equality for all!" until late in the evening. Despite directives from the Police Department to keep a minimal distance of 50 feet from the entrance to the campus, demonstrators continued to break through the line to intimidate students, faculty and visitors as they drove onto the campus. While there had been no violence, the mere presence of the protestors distracted many of the faculty and school's administration from their daily activities, over worry of a potential riot erupting on campus. After the national media left, it wasn't long before the group became disinterested with their activities and disbanded. But they made their point. The media had given them free national publicity. David Gambrell hoped that this crisis would end soon. But there would be more to follow.

The President's national security adviser sat in the Oval Office, waiting for William Duncan to arrive. Aaron Crosby had

127

requested another meeting to discuss the President's intent to recommend U.N. sanctions against Israel. He was disturbed by his sudden announcement shortly after their last meeting.

Aaron's relationship with the President went back to their childhood. The two grew up going to the same Church, attending high school and playing on the football team together. Both even pursued the same major in college; political science. It was this unique camaraderie that led Duncan to ask Aaron to serve as his national security advisor. This wasn't an appointment based on mere friendship, however. Aaron entered the military after college, and then served two terms as a United States congressman before joining the President's team of advisers. In spite of their relationship, he had remained at a respectful distance from the President aside from his official duties; until now.

President Duncan entered the office. He wondered what the nature of this meeting was since the two had met just yesterday afternoon. "Good morning, Aaron," he welcomed Crosby, as the adviser stood up. "Good morning, Mr. President," Aaron Crosby returned the greeting. "Oh, please, we're friends." Duncan appreciated the respect he was always given by his security adviser, but also valued the close friendship that the two had held over the years. Aaron waited for the President to be seated before he returned to his chair. "I came to discuss our position regarding the standoff between Israel and the Palestinians," the national security adviser got right to the point. "I'm assuming you're referring to my recent press release," President Duncan speculated. "That would be the case, and it gives me reason for deep concern." Aaron looked directly at the President as he spoke. "I see no reason for concern at all," the President tried to convince his adviser. "We must do all we can to prevent a regional conflict. This action is necessary to force them to be careful in how they respond to aggression." Aaron was even more disturbed over the President's comments than he was when he had first heard about his intentions to recommend sanctions against Israel.

"Mr. President-Bill, if I may speak freely, our approach to Israel's defense could have long lasting effects on our own security." The President looked up with a start. "And how is that?" he quizzed Aaron. The security adviser took a deep breath before continuing. "Go back and look at Israel's start as a nation," he suggested. "Do you remember the Abrahamic Covenant?" President Duncan was irritated. He was meeting with his national security adviser because of an international concern. "I know what the Bible says all about that blessing and cursing stuff, but we have a potential all-out war in the middle-east," he ranted. "And you came to warn me against standing up to Israel because of a Bible story that was written 3,500 years ago?" [28] His voice was getting louder, but he stopped short.

The door to the Congressional Prayer Room was open as Congressmen Edwards and Wilson walked from the Rotunda of the Capitol Building into the small chapel. "Good morning, gentlemen," Chaplain Cartwright stood when he saw the congressmen. "Good morning, Chaplain," the two lawmakers returned his greeting as they shook his hand. The small room had six chairs, and was trimmed in a manner that would not be offensive to any Church affiliation. But its decorations reflected the national belief in God and His place throughout the history of America. A stained glass window portrayed an image of George Washington as he knelt in prayer. And the words of the Psalmist read: *"Preserve me, O God, for in Thee do I put my trust."* Psalm 16:1.

Chris and the Speaker of the House sat down, and the chaplain pulled a chair around to face them. "Thank you for joining me today," he said appreciatively. "I was beginning to think that it was going to be just me." A.J. Wilson smiled. "I have to confess that I almost didn't come," he admitted. "I'm sure the room would be packed if this was a social gathering, but what I have in mind is more important," the chaplain reflected. "I would like to take this prayer a step farther than our weekly chapel. But first, you tell me, what is your own purpose for showing up today?" he asked the two lawmakers. Congressman Edwards was thoughtful for a moment. "I want to see unity in the House," he reflected. "Yes, and throughout every branch of the government," Wilson added. "Then let's allow that to be the focus of this morning's time of prayer," the chaplain suggested. "And as our daily prayer begins to grow, let's also pray specifically for the President, that he would have a heart for God." The chaplain paused to allow the two congressmen to reflect on each prayer request. "President Duncan is continually pulled by tremendous forces that can easily cause him to lose sight of this country's godly values. So let's pray for Divine guidance in every aspect of his daily duties."

Chaplain Cartwright turned and knelt down at his chair. The three began to pray, and the chaplain prayed aloud. It wasn't a written or prepared prayer, but was a prayer of spontaneity, and with a passion the two congressmen had never before heard from his lips.

Scott walked back to his office from the Fellowship Hall with a fresh cup of coffee, where he found Kelly Graham talking with Connie. He had intended to call her to discuss the latest developments regarding the school concerns that Kelly was faithfully following. "Mind if I join you?" he asked the two

130

women as he pulled up a chair and sat down. "Not at all," Kelly replied. "You may want to hear what we're talking about. Let me go ahead and spill it. Things are going a little too far with this school thing," she continued. "I agree with you completely," Scott concurred. "Did Connie tell you about Jordan's grade on his report because of its Christian theme?" Kelly nodded. "Yes, and that's not all. Mr. Williams just gave me this." She handed Scott the book she had received from the school principal. Scott read the title, *A Perverted Gospel*. "What's this?" he frowned. "A new anti-Christian group has received a court approval to have this distributed in our schools. Mr. Williams' hands are tied," she explained. "Yes, but ours aren't," the pastor interjected. "I'm just a little uncertain about how far I should go with my own involvement." Kelly continued. "When I accepted my place as the PTA president, I never thought I would be dealing with these kinds of issues. Speaking out against the first incident seemed like the right thing to do, but I just wonder if anything *can* be done?"

Scott considered her question for a moment, and then replied. "This is much deeper than a simple misunderstanding between parents and teachers-and other religions. It's a spiritual battle for the souls of our children, and not just in Blue Ridge Heights; it's happening all across America." Kelly agreed with the pastor. "What's happening in our town is what we normally see on the evening news, and we may see this situation on the news before it's over." He spoke with a concerned voice. "Maybe God has placed you-maybe all of us, in this town for this very purpose. While it would be easy to turn our heads and act like it never happened, being a leader doesn't give us the privilege to avoid sticky issues. It gives us a greater responsibility to face them," he exhorted her. "Then what should we do next?" Kelly inquired. "If you're willing to take this step,

I think the only thing left to do is take this issue to court," the pastor suggested. Kelly agreed. "I know someone who may be able to help," he volunteered. "Let me make a telephone call, and I'll be in touch." Kelly shook the pastor's hand appreciatively as she stood to leave. She felt reassured knowing that someone of his influence was standing behind her, in whatever might lie ahead.

Back at the White House, President Duncan had been in conference with Aaron Crosby for nearly an hour. Meetings with his security adviser normally lasted no longer than thirty minutes. The President was already late for a scheduled meeting with the Vice President, but he wanted to see just where Aaron's little homily was leading. He was partly annoyed, but amazed at his adviser's suggestion that America's future could possibly be affected by its relationship with Israel.

"There is no imminent danger from a security point of view. But maybe even our nation's present economic condition is a result of our policy toward Israel," Aaron contended. "So, you really believe that the blessing and curses that were mentioned to Abraham, all the way back in the Bible include us today?" President Duncan asked, cynically. Aaron was about to reply, but Duncan cut him short. "I tell you what. Maybe you should focus on national security, and leave God out of the picture." Aaron was shocked at the President's words. He was William Duncan's close personal friend and adviser, but right now he felt like an outsider. He had spoken his convictions; he had given a qualified briefing, and now was being ridiculed. Aaron exited the room quietly. The President watched him leave, and tried to forget what he had just been told.

Scott Crawford had barely completed his telephone conversation with Chris Edwards when the phone began ringing in the front office again. "Trinity Christian Fellowship," Connie answered. It was Wesley Crenshaw on the other end. "I was wondering if you and the pastor are free for lunch?" the Church member asked her cordially. "I believe we are," Connie replied. "Where would you like to meet?" she asked. "I'm in Greenville right now, so maybe we could meet about half-way?" Connie told him they would leave shortly, and they agreed to meet at the Smokehouse Café in thirty minutes.

Wesley was already seated when Scott and Connie arrived. He stood to greet them when he saw them approaching his table. "How are my pastor and his lovely wife doing today?" he said, in his usual charming manner. After exchanging greetings they sat down and placed their orders. Wesley only ordered a glass of tea, but said, "You go ahead and eat. I had a late breakfast." Scott thought it strange for the businessman to ask them out for a lunch meeting when he wasn't going to eat, himself. Wesley was always ready to share the details of his work with anyone who had the time to listen. Although he wasn't aware of this, it always seemed as if his money was the most important thing in his life. Scott smiled. *He's very passionate about his work,*" he thought to himself. But today there was something deeper that the pastor couldn't quite put his finger on.

Their orders finally arrived at the table. As they continued to converse, Scott and Connie began to sense a change in Wesley's disposition. He stopped talking for a few moments, and finally spoke again. "Something has been bothering me for some time, and I need to share it with you." They waited, expectantly to find out what was troubling him.

"There's been a change in your preaching," he said, sipping on his tea. "I hope it's for the better," Scott responded, curious as to why his preaching had become a matter of concern to the businessman. "Well, I'm not concerned about how you're preaching, but *what* you've been preaching," Wesley prodded on. "I must say that I've left feeling uncomfortable for the last several weeks." Scott stopped chewing and swallowed his food. "I'm glad to hear that," he said, bluntly. "My job as a pastor is not to tell my congregation what they want to hear, but what they-what *we* need to hear." Wesley had not expected Scott to respond in this manner. "Let me be clear," he spoke back sharply. "Your job is to preach the Bible, not to single out Church members, or rally the school against the public school system, or," he persisted, "to involve yourselves with politics."

Scott now realized why his parishioner had called the meeting. He had dreaded sitting down and talking with Karen and Wesley about Karen's classroom issues, and should have done it earlier. But he was taken aback by something else. "Please clarify something," Scott requested. "What have I said that makes you feel that I have singled anyone out in my preaching?" The wealthy Church member hesitated before responding. "I'm talking about my son, Timothy. While he was in college he confessed to the Church that he was gay before moving away. Our family has felt out of place in the Church since that day." This was the first that Scott had ever heard anything about his Church member's son. "I was not even aware of this." Scott hesitated for a moment as he prayed for the right words. "You are not responsible for the choices that your grown son makes with his life; and your Church family would never hold that against you," he tried to persuade Wesley. "Now, about my preaching," the pastor steered back to Wesley's sharp challenge. "Pastors of smaller congregations have an extra heavy burden on their shoulders. When we have to address a difficult subject, sometimes it feels as if everyone is just guessing who we're talking about," he continued. "Sometimes it's even

134

tempted to avoid issues that may be offensive to someone in the audience. But as for Timothy, this just isn't the case."

Wesley changed the subject. "In reading the Bible," the businessman lowered his voice, "we need to be careful what we say to others; I mean, Jesus said that whoever speaks against the Holy Spirit, it will not be forgiven him." Scott was a little confused at what the Church member had just said. "I don't know how my preaching can be interpreted as speaking against the Holy Spirit," he started to say, but Wesley held up his hand and said, "Let me finish. Karen's teaching is her ministry, and your opposition to her work is a hindrance to how God could use her."

Scott's heart was pounding. *"How could Karen's criticism of Christianity in the classroom be described as 'ministry'?"* he thought to himself. He started to speak, but decided to hear Wesley through. "If Karen should be removed from her class, it would take a light out of her classroom," he said in an authoritative voice. "Jesus said that it would be better for you to be thrown into the sea with a millstone around your neck, than to offend his children." [30]

Scott could remain silent no longer. "Wesley," he spoke up. "The Bible is like a land surveyor's reference. If he loses his location, he must return to the starting point or his measurements will be inaccurate. The Bible is the beginning-and end of all truth. I cannot stray from it, no matter how uncomfortable it may make you feel." Wesley slid his chair back, preparing to stand up. "We have enjoyed a strong fellowship with the Church family for many years," he said, ignoring the pastor's last remark. "But I can no longer sit under your ministry if it continues to move in the direction that you've been leading." He stopped speaking. The silence was deafening as Scott sensed that he was sending him a stronger message; *"The Church is a small congregation. I could lose my salary."* Wesley stood up to leave. Scott started to put his hand on the meal ticket; he couldn't accept the man's generosity under these circumstances. But Wesley took it and left the table to pay the bill.

The pastor's heart pounded harder as he looked at Connie, waiting for Wesley to leave the restaurant. His faith was being tested. The expression on Connie's face told him to *"keep standing, and I'll stand with you, regardless of the outcome."*

Later that evening, the small group of congressional collaborators was meeting in a conference room in the Rayburn Office Building. Looking back, Edwards was pleased with the progress he felt had been made on their resolution over the last two months-in spite of all the opposition it had received. The three men, Congressmen Edwards, Campbell and Graham Gillespie had already discussed the final draft, written by Edwards and Campbell. Amy Patterson had withdrawn her support from the proposal and was not present. The congressmen agreed to present the completed proposal to the Speaker of the House to be introduced to the entire House of Representatives.

They left the meeting in silence. Each one felt a sense of being a part of something much bigger than anything that had gone to the House floor in decades; something that could restore integrity to the nation. But they also understood that their willingness, or insistence to push for these strong measures could cost them their offices. *"This resolution will create many questions that can only be answered or solved by God Himself,"* Edwards thought quietly. If by some chance any constitutional amendments were to pass both houses of Congress, it was certain to be challenged in court.

Marvin Maddox sat at the anchor desk. He finished reviewing the evening broadcast agenda and then rested for a few minutes with his eyes closed. It was his personal practice to clear his mind quietly before each broadcast. The bright spotlights turned on overhead, and camera operators assumed their positions behind the cameras. He faced the camera, now ready to begin as the clock counted backwards from five to one.

"Good evening, and welcome to Wednesday's broadcast of the UBC Evening News," Maddox glanced at his computer monitor. Tonight, we will revisit the drama that continues to unfold on Capitol Hill. We recently reported the introduction of House Resolution 291, sponsored by Congresswoman Sara Jackson. This bill, specifically aimed at Churches and Christian non-profit organizations, would expand the nation's hate crime laws to impose severe penalties to Churches, pastors, and nonprofits who openly criticize anyone living together outside of what they define as biblical marriage. The sponsors of this bill believe that the Church's position is purely traditional, and hold to outdated beliefs that are hostile to modern society."

The anchorman was uncomfortable about having to provide repeated coverage of this bill, and was looking forward to announcing his next item. "But for the longest, unbeknown to Sara Jackson and her constituents, a select group from within the Constitution Party was also working on a measure that could deliver the death blow to her bill. Their proposal, called the *Heritage and Freedom Amendments Act*, would actually amend the U.S. Constitution to embrace a radical return to the nation's historical conservative roots. This could be the turning of a new day in America."

The musical theme began playing in the background as the camera zoomed out to show a distant view of the anchorman as he concluded the evening report. Members of the production team smiled at Marvin Maddox's bold move to report the Edwards Bill in such a positive light. Harold Gentry however, stood behind the glass window in the control room glowering, with his arms folded. He turned and walked quickly back to his office.

Ellen Duncan walked up the grand staircase in the White House to the executive residence. She was returning from a two week tour of public schools throughout the northeastern region of the United States, advocating for her personal focus as the first lady; abstinence before marriage. Her "true love waits" campaign had been ridiculed by many who said that hers was a personal issue that had no place in the public arena. Her argument was that today's teens were flooded with sexually explicit propaganda through public media, advertising and the movie industry, with little or no attention to the virtues of remaining sexually pure before marriage. It was no wonder that society had been flooded by a staggering number of teen pregnancies, abortions and STDs.

Changing this mindset was the first lady's passion. Just before leaving for college two years ago, their daughter had broken down and told them that she had just received an abortion. Miraculously, it had stayed out of the news. Ellen's mother instinct could feel the silent pain that her daughter was living with, even though she didn't speak it.

Arming herself with the facts, the first lady embarked on a campaign to educate the nation's youth: While abortion rates had declined over the last several decades, about 750,000 teens were getting pregnant each year. Over 200,000 of these pregnancies were aborted. And about eighty percent of women receiving an abortion were single; this resulted in a vicious cycle of poverty, illiteracy, and dependence on welfare. This sobering fact cost American tax payers billions of dollars annually. Out of all these figures, hundreds of thousands of teens and young mothers were living with physical, emotional, and spiritual scars, with no one to turn to; something that could be prevented. The first lady was indeed a spiritually sensitive person, and held to high moral standards. She strongly felt that if she could do her part in shaping the hearts and minds of the nation's youth, this trend could be reversed.

Ellen walked down the center hall and glanced inside the sitting room where her husband was leaning back in a recliner, staring blankly at the wall. He seemed distant, as if something was disturbing him; the President usually spoke as soon as he saw his wife each afternoon, whether he or she was the first to reach the executive residence.

"What's bothering you?" she asked the President. William Duncan sighed as he looked toward the first lady. "I shouldn't be discussing this," he responded, "but in my personal briefing this morning, Aaron totally overstepped his bounds." Ellen raised her eyebrows, interested. "How could he do that?" The President leaned forward, resting his elbows in his lap. "I mean, he had the audacity to tell me I was mistaken in my stand toward Israel, and get this; he based his concerns on a story from the Bible!" he replied with a note of sarcasm. Ellen smiled. She knew that her husband, who was not as spiritually sensitive as Aaron, was feeling challenged by his adviser's suggestion. "Let me guess," she speculated. "Was it Abraham?" Duncan looked back at his wife without speaking. "Well, in the strictest sense, he does have a point," she conjectured. The President struggled with his thoughts. "But my job is to lead the country by standards of the law, not religious beliefs," he argued.

Ellen had been massaging her husband's shoulders gently. She stopped to look him in his eyes. "What's so wrong about letting the Bible influence our daily lives?" she asked pointedly. "After all, what good is it if it's not good enough to live by? Just remember this," she said gently. "You didn't appoint Aaron on the basis of your relationship alone. He's in his position because you had confidence in his qualifications. Trust your instincts." She turned and walked out of the room, leaving the President reflecting on her words.

Darrell Youngblood arrived at the NASE office earlier than usual this morning. A legal meeting was scheduled later in the day to lay out their course of action against King University. He hadn't heard back from Marcus Jefferson; something was missing in this case. As committed as he was to represent any claims of discrimination, they didn't need to pursue this one without a solid case. After all, King was an internationally known institution. While NASE's cause would benefit greatly if they won a lawsuit, it could severely hurt their cause if they lost. As he went through his notes, Ronald Sherman, the research coordinator knocked on the door and walked in his office. "Something's just not right about the King University case," he told his associate as he sat down. "Why?" his associate asked. "I'd just rather not hold this afternoon's strategy session if we don't have all the facts." Ronald looked confused. "I still don't understand?" he hoped for more clarification. "Marcus Jefferson has some valid concerns," the director of NASE replied. "But we still don't have any students who can support his allegations. I don't know if we should risk pursuing this one."

He noticed that Ronald had a slight smile on his face. "What is it? Are you holding back on something?" Darrell queried. "We might can pursue it, even without Marcus' testimony," the executive sat forward in his chair, interested. "While I was digging into the University President's background; his name is David Gambrell," Ronald began sharing, "I discovered a few interesting relationships." Darrell was fully

140

engaged by his associate's words. "David Gambrell is from Blue Ridge Heights, South Carolina," Ronald paused to read the expression on Darrell's face. "That's Congressman Chris Edwards' hometown. They grew up together in this little Church, Trinity Christian Fellowship." The director still didn't seem to get the connection. "But there's more," Ronald continued. "Wesley Crenshaw, the technology business magnate, is also a member of this Church." Darrell continued listening, with interest.

"Let's take a completely different approach," Ronald proposed. "Crenshaw's corporation employs several thousand workers. It's well-known that he is an openly conservative Christian, and a strong financial supporter of the university. If we go after his company, that might affect King University," he concluded. Darrell was quiet for a moment. "Let me think about it, and I'll let you know," he said thoughtfully.

Scott Crawford had begun to anticipate his telephone conversations with his mentor, Russell Taylor. The two were now talking weekly, both to keep the elder minister updated on the increasingly exciting events in South Carolina, and to simply encourage each other. Today, their conversation had lasted longer than usual. Rev. Taylor sensed the anguish in Scott's voice as he shared the confrontation between him and his well-to-do Church member. In his many years of ministry, he had encountered several painful experiences with Church members whom he loved, but still resulted in a separation of their relationships.

"From what I gather," the retired pastor spoke after Scott unloaded this burden on him, "your wealthy Church member has a lifetime history in your community. That means he has roots, and sooner or later, he may return. Don't give up on him." Scott was encouraged by the elder minister's admonition. He was still nursing some strong emotions from his recent confrontation with Wesley, but agreed not give up on his wandering sheep too soon.

The lights had just been turned out at the Edwards' house when the telephone rang. Chris rolled over and picked up the receiver on the night stand. "Hello?" he answered, wondering who would be calling so late. "Chris, you'd better sit down," Congressman Campbell was on the other end. The younger congressman sat up and turned on the lamp. "There's been a national catastrophe," Campbell informed him. "What?" Chris responded, in disbelief. Nancy heard the tone of his voice, and sat up to listen. "It was the Charleston Cougars game. A bomb went off about ten minutes ago and they fear thousands were killed!" The Charleston Cougars was a new professional baseball team in Charleston, South Carolina. The team was averaging twenty five thousand spectators per game in this first season.

A knot began building up in Chris' stomach as he discussed the crisis with the other congressman. Nancy heard her cell phone ringing in the living room; her instinct told her it was related to the call her husband was on. She hurried out of the bedroom to answer it as Chris continued talking with the other congressman. Chris hung up and began putting on a shirt. Nancy was ending her call when he walked out into the living room. She sat on the couch, quiet.

"There's been a possible terrorist attack in Charleston," Chris informed Nancy. "I was just talking with my director," she nodded, still shaken by the news. "Have you been called in?" he asked, understanding that his wife's job called her to action in case of such a disaster. "Not yet," Nancy replied as she stood back up. "The executive committee is meeting right now, and I'll know within the hour." The congressman held his wife in his arms quietly for a moment; he knew they might be separated for several days. I've been called for a national security meeting at the Capitol," he finally said. The couple knew it would be a long night. Chris finished getting dressed, and prepared to leave.

Sirens were screaming all over Charleston South Carolina. The night sky was lit up from a massive fire rising from what remained standing of the baseball stadium. A row of fire trucks were already on the scene where three massive explosions had occurred an hour earlier. Another one slowly drove into a large parking lot filled with emergency response vehicles and people standing back from the fire. Lights were flashing for blocks around the scene of the bombing. Several dozen casualties were covered with sheets on the side parking lot. A makeshift triage area had been set up on the end of the parking lot farther away from the stadium where over one hundred spectators with serious injuries lay on blankets waiting to be treated. Others with minor injuries were sitting up, still in shock from the explosions.

Jason McCall, the fire chief stood near his command vehicle speaking with the police chief and a crime scene investigator. "Has the cause been determined yet?" he asked the chief hurriedly. He could get a better idea at the best way to fight the flames if he knew whether it was a known gas leak or some other sort of explosion. "We've ruled out a gas leak, the police chief replied. "No one's gotten in there yet, but my guess is, terrorism. There could be as many as twenty five thousand casualties." The three emergency responders were interrupted by another fire truck approaching; Jason began to walk toward it. "Keep me posted," he told the police chief.

The police chief tried to make his way closer to the ruins of the stadium for a closer look, but the heat from the inferno forced him back. It was a sobering thought that thousands of lives had been snuffed out in just a moment's time by some unknown evil force. Throughout the night he worked tirelessly to coordinate with his police officers and dozens of other emergency responders. As the sun began to rise, more trucks arrived and were pouring water toward the fire, leaving a large cloud of smoky steam around the blaze; many more were lined up, ready to move in their place. Long hoses interlaced each other, with water streaming all over the parking lot. All emergency responders were already exhausted, but knew it would be several days, before they could return home.

After breakfast, Jordan and Brianna Crenshaw ran out the door to head for the bus stop. They were tired of the comments that students had been throwing at them about their father's stand involving Jordan's assignments. Several had even posted hurtful notes online about the two preacher's kids, even though most of their classmates were standing behind them. They had been instructed to avoid any controversy if at all possible; their parents would deal with the online bullying in the proper manner. Hopefully, none of the trouble-makers would be on the bus.

Scott Crawford poured a cup of coffee and went into the living room to turn on the morning news. As he sat down, the morning anchorman was standing outside the Charleston Sports Arena with a blazing fire in the background. The young pastor leaned forward so he could hear the report. He was stunned by the news that thousands of baseball fans had been killed in a terrorist attack just hours earlier. "It is still too early to investigate from inside of what just yesterday was the Charleston Sports Arena," the reporter announced. "But preliminary reports believe that it was a bombing from an undisclosed terrorist group. Our news correspondent is at the nation's Capitol where Senator

Randall Smith, the Constitution Party's presidential candidate will give a statement, shortly." Scott wondered where Congressman Edwards was at the moment, and hoped to talk with him soon.

The scene on the television screen switched to the Rotunda of the U.S. Capitol building where Senator Randall Smith approached a podium with numerous microphones mounted to its front. As he began speaking Scott could see Chris Edwards standing in the background, talking with a group of other congressmen. "Senator Smith, what should the proper response be to this disaster?" a field reporter asked the presidential candidate. "First of all, we must make sure that everyone involved in the recovery is protected in case of another explosion," he addressed his interviewer. "Due to the magnitude of the disaster, it could take weeks to clear and recover all casualties. Before developing a plan for response, we must first identify the perpetrators of this horrific act. Let us all pray for the comfort on the families of these victims, and that God would restore this land." The scene switched back to the news studio where the morning anchorman continued his program. *"His response demonstrates qualities of a good leader,"* Crawford thought to himself. As shocking as this event was to the entire nation, these concerns would be resting heavily on his small town, too. The young pastor began to prepare his mind for the right message to deliver to his congregation on Sunday morning.

10

Future Uncertainties

The office of Godwin & Associates was quiet. Jeff Godwin's two partners were engaged in a lengthy court hearing, leaving him alone for the afternoon. The distinguished attorney sat behind his desk reviewing his most pressing cases when his administrative assistant walked in and laid a newspaper on his desk. "Here's something you might be interested in," she said before returning to her desk. The attorney's passion lay in helping individuals whose religious liberties were being threatened. He looked up from his reading to glance at the local headlines. It immediately got his attention. The attorney picked up the paper to get a second glance. It read, *"School District Faces Continued Woes."* He leaned back in his chair and began reading:

"A conflict that began in the classroom of a neighboring school district has developed tension between classroom, the school district office, and a host of angry parents. It all started several months

back when Karen Crenshaw, a teacher at Blue
Ridge Heights Academy introduced a lesson on
 comparing major world religions, but left details of
Christianity out of her lesson. The teacher, who ironically
did so because she wanted to avoid conflict, inadvertently
sparked a dispute that spread to the school district
office. Mrs. Crenshaw also delivered
a failing grade to one of her students for doing
a report using a Christian theme. Interestingly,
this student was the son of her pastor, and
the family appealed the decision to the school
district office. The school board is standing
behind the teacher's decision.

But to make matters worse, the same school
 district informed its schools that a booklet entitled,
"A Perverted Gospel," published by a newly
emerging anti-Christian organization, will be
distributed to all high school students in the
upcoming semester. This book, that paints Jesus
as a child molester was given approval of the
courts to be distributed to balance fairness in the
annual distribution of New Testaments to public
school students. The entire community is in an
uproar. It has been rumored that the PTA is
considering legal action on behalf of both issues."

The attorney raised his eyebrows. Congressman Edwards
had recently called him to tell him about this same issue. He had
intended to look into it later on in the week. *"Maybe I should go
ahead and give the PTA officials a call?"* he considered
thoughtfully.

Members of the university board of directors began
gathering in the Administration Building at King University. The
board met twice each year, but had been called in for an

148

emergency meeting in response to the recent attacks on the university. Jesse Wood sat down at the head of the long conference table and the other members took their seats preparing for the meeting to start. He began thumbing through a sheaf of papers in front of him. "Since we last spoke, the school has received yet, another blow," Wood announced. "This one could be more damaging." The chairman began passing a stack of folders around the table for each member to take one.

"Let's go ahead and get the big item out of the way," he suggested. "The IRS has launched a discrimination investigation against the school. This regards our policy that requires students to hold to a Christian testimony," the chairman continued. "So, what's the worst possible outcome?" Gary Pace, the board secretary asked. "If we are found in violation of any statutes, the school could face a heavy fine, or lose its exempt status." Rick Hamby, another board member leaned back in his chair. "Perhaps we should consider some changes to our policy," he suggested. "That should stop any further action." "Yes," Gary agreed.

"Just a moment," Jesse spoke up. "Keep in mind that this is a Christian institution, and our duty is to uphold its biblical values." Most board meetings were carried out as a matter of mere formality. The most pressing matter was usually the annual budget, or new staff appointments. There was normally little or no disagreement of any significance between the members. But today, there was noticeable tension between Gary and Rick, and the remaining members. They had expected to adjourn by lunch time, but it was more likely to turn into an all day meeting.

The sky over Charleston was a smoky gray from the massive plumes of smoke that soared menacingly through the sky. A thick haze drifted throughout the city. It had been nearly thirty-six hours since the bombing. The fire was nearly contained,

149

and emergency coordinators were preparing to begin the recovery process soon. Miraculously, two thousand fans were outside of the stadium area going to the concession stands, or coming or going to their vehicles when the explosions occurred, and survived. Of those closest to the stadium, nearly four hundred had been taken to local hospitals with serious to life-threatening injuries.

Nancy Edwards pulled into the parking lot with several emergency volunteer workers from Emergency Preparedness International and parked in a section marked for emergency workers. Her job was to oversee the efforts of several emergency response teams as they arrived. She got out of her car and headed toward a picture of total chaos. The lifeless bodies of dozens of victims lay in rows, covered by sheets. And dozens more who were injured remained on the parking lot being assisted by emergency medical personnel as they waited to be taken to the hospital. A crowd of spectators stood on the street, restrained by a row of national guardsmen. An officer approached Nancy and pointed her toward the command post after seeing her identification.

Before addressing the workers, she asked the officer to brief her on the teams who were already there. Within thirty minutes her three teams of relief workers began going through the parking lot, carrying drinks to weary firemen, paramedics, and the countless survivors from the bombing, and assisting victims to stretchers. The flames were beginning to die down, and hot coals smoldered throughout the stadium. Most of the outer wall was still standing, and about half of the stadium seating area remained intact in three separate sections. Steamy vapors rose from the ground, slowly replacing the dark billows of smoke that had covered the town for the better part of the day. A sickening feeling came over Nancy as she looked into the stadium area where thousands of lifeless bodies lay in the stands that stood precariously. She could hear the moans and cries of persons who were critically wounded, but could not be rescued because of the danger in reaching them. Countless others lay beneath the rubble. The stairwells leading out of the stadium were full of the bodies of spectators who had not made it. *"Perhaps from a last minute effort to escape?"* Nancy wondered. Firemen dressed in full heat-resistant garb began to file cautiously into the arena to begin the long process of rescue and recovery. Several large trailers with, "Mass Casualty Unit" printed on the sides were lining up to aid in the process. It would be at least another day before inspectors could get close enough to the main section of the stadium to make sure it was safe enough to enter. Nancy turned away from the scene. She knew she had to regain her composure in order to effectively coordinate with all others participating in the relief efforts.

It had been a hectic day at the UBC Studio in Washington, DC. Marvin Maddox remained behind the camera most of the day, giving continued coverage of developments at the site of the disaster in Charleston. One hour of continuous broadcast speaking was the emotional equivalent of an eight hour day of physical labor. Already, he had spoken continuously for four hours with very few station breaks, and would be returning to the studio in thirty minutes. The middle-aged anchorman sat behind his desk with his eyes closed, trying to release the tension from his day when Harold Gentry walked in his office. He dropped a folder on Marvin's desk and sat down in the chair across from him. "Hard day?" he asked the exhausted anchorman. He had spent 10 years as an anchor before his move as news director at UBC headquarters. Not having to stay behind the camera was less stressful to him, while allowing him to play a direct role in the daily broadcast. "I'm just decompressing for a few minutes before I go back on air," Marvin replied, leaning forward in his office chair.

"What's this?" he asked, as he glanced at the folder. "That," Harold replied, "was supposed to be the news item of the year, until the bombing." Marvin opened the folder and tilted his glasses down so he could read the print. "We've already talked about Congressman Edwards. The story about him harassing his executive assistant, and probably even more is really big," the news director continued, standing back up. "I'd like to see this as the headliner for the evening broadcast. If it comes after the Charleston attack, it won't be remembered by anyone." He turned to leave Marvin's office. "Doesn't this need to go through research department?" Marvin asked. "I got it straight from the girl involved," Harold turned back to face his anchorman. "No research needed."

Marvin took a deep breath. "I won't do it," he said firmly. Gentry stopped, angered that his authority had just been challenged. He leaned forward, resting his hands on the anchorman's desk. "I ought to fire you right now," he said forcefully. Marvin looked his news director squarely in the eyes. The tension between the two had been rising steadily over the past several weeks; this was the last straw. "That won't be necessary," he shot back before Harold had barely gotten the threat out of his mouth. He opened a desk drawer and began removing some personal items, placing them on the desk top, his heart pounding. "Just a minute, you can't leave without a notice." The news director realized he had spoken in the heat of his emotion. "And you couldn't terminate me without cause." Harold tried to back off his challenge, but the anchorman continued packing his personal belongings. "Without my recommendation, you'll never find another job in broadcasting," Harold retorted, and stormed out of the office.

The elevator door opened on the basement level of the West Wing of the White House, and President Duncan stepped out into the open hall. He was accompanied by his chief of staff, and a secret service agent who escorted the two officials down the corridor. They continued to an open door leading into the Situation Room. The agent waited in the hall guarding the entrance to the room. The Situation Room was a massive conference complex and secure communications command center. Here, the President was briefed by his national security team during all foreign and domestic crises. Large flat screens flanked the walls, and an enormous video screen was mounted at the end of a conference table with six executive chairs lining each side. After news of the bombing in Charleston early that morning, President Duncan cancelled all appointments for the remainder of the day. His chief of staff scheduled a video conference with the governor of South Carolina so they could communicate face to face about the latest developments as they took place.

The President sat down at the end of the table and received a report from the director of homeland security. Aaron Crosby sat directly on the President's right. Key members of his staff filled the other chairs. It seemed to Aaron that President Duncan was intentionally avoiding eye contact with him. The President recalled their earlier conversation the instant he learned about the bombing in Charleston. *"Could this really be connected to the proposed sanctions against Israel?"* the President wondered, trying to hide that he was shaken by the incident.

Mike Blackwell, the general manager at UBC Headquarters in Washington listened through the telephone receiver as Harold unloaded an emotional string of complaints. The general manager was responsible for the overall operations at UBC headquarters, and played an integral role in making sure it maintained a stable financial status. He believed that the anchorman was largely responsible for the station's high ratings in the broadcasting industry. Mike had observed a quiet tension between his news director and Marvin Maddox. Harold claimed that Marvin willfully disregarded corporate policies. If this was so, maybe his sudden resignation was for the best. But then, Mike was troubled by Gentry's frequent emotional outbursts. Somehow it just didn't add up. The news director might have been the real reason his respected anchor had quit. "On top of it all, he stormed out in the middle of a national crisis," the news director ranted. "Just call in one of the backups for tonight's program," Mike advised Harold. "We can meet tomorrow morning to discuss a replacement," he said before hanging up.

Late that evening Nancy Edwards swiped the plastic pass card to open her motel room door. For the past two days she had arrived at the disaster site before 5:30 AM and returned to her room long after dark. Although physically and emotionally exhausted, her passion for her work drove her to keep going. Nancy had trained dozens of emergency executives to be prepared in the event of such a catastrophe. Nothing could have prepared her for what she faced upon arrival at the site of the bombing. In spite of the devastation, somehow, several thousand spectators had miraculously survived the terrorist attack. The casualties could have numbered over twenty five thousand, but the final count was estimated at nearly fifteen thousand. It was still the largest mass casualty disaster that had ever occurred on American soil.

Before showering, the Congressman's wife turned on the television to catch the latest news coverage. When she found the UBC news channel, another anchor was in the place where Marvin Maddox usually sat. "Another scandal from Washington has just been unearthed that could pose a serious threat to pending House measures, as well as the Constitution Party's fight for the upcoming presidential elections," he reported. "In a stunning blow to conservatives, allegations of sexual harassment have been brought against Congressman Christopher Edwards by his executive assistant, Jessica James." Nancy caught her breath. She burst into tears as the report continued. "Edwards is the junior sponsor of the Constitution Party's pending *Heritage and Freedom Amendments Act* that actually calls for House and Senate ethics reform. If proven true, these accusations could be the death blow to this landmark piece of legislation."

The congressman's wife buried her head in her hands, in shock. Nancy and Chris had always had an open relationship with each other. There was never any reason not to trust him. But the impact of this news threw her off completely. *"How could I not have known?"* she cried to herself. Her cell phone rang, and she reached in her pocketbook to answer it. It was Rebecca Hudson, Senator Hudson's wife. "Nancy," Rebecca was relieved she had answered. She could tell that Nancy was crying; her friend realized she had already heard the news. "What you just heard isn't true." Nancy began to calm down. "What?" she asked, wiping her face. "Will just told me that Chris is the victim of a political scandal," Rebecca continued. "They think that someone is trying to throw the presidential elections."

Nancy was overwhelmed. First, the national news had just reported that Chris had been harassing a staff member. *"His*

155

executive assistant!" she thought. Now, before having time to process this news, she had been told it was just a scandal. He was being used. "I don't know what to think," she confessed to her friend. "Politics can be a vicious world," Rebecca reminded her. "Trust me. I've seen it all." She stopped talking to allow Nancy to process it for a moment. "I tell you what," she finally said gently. Let's meet for lunch tomorrow. My treat." Nancy hung up the phone quietly. She wanted to think Chris was innocent, but just didn't know what to believe at the moment. *"How can anyone go through this?"* she asked herself. *"If this is the way Congress does business, it's no wonder our nation is in such a mess."*

Wesley Crenshaw had driven to Charleston to check on the Bay City location's operations after news of the devastating bombing. The office was located less than a mile from where the bombs went off. Even though windows had been blown out of buildings for blocks around, his location had been unharmed. Since his employees were not at risk, he returned to the upstate the next day. Now, he prepared to meet with Jase Childers before launching the campaign to introduce their new Intele-phone. They had worked for months in preparation for the campaign launch. The management team was projecting the initial shipments of their new computerized telephone to sell out as soon as it was released.

"Come in," Wesley greeted his executive. Jase entered the room and sat down close to his employer's desk. "I can't tell you how long I've waited for this day," Wesley told his marketing manager. "This could be the product that moves us ahead of the major competition." Jase cleared his throat uncomfortably. "Yes sir, we share your excitement," he said to Wesley. "But there's a recent development with our advertising

156

client that you may need to know about before we launch." Wesley looked up, wondering what he was about to hear. "UBC News Headquarters has just lost their evening anchor, Marvin Maddox. Since his replacement, their stock value has fallen considerably," the marketing executive explained. "What was the reason for his leaving?" Wesley asked. As anxious as he was to launch their new product, he knew that if the station's ratings fell too much, this could adversely affect the release of their new product. "The word is out that it was political. Maddox refused to report on the scandal about Congressman Edwards, and walked out." Wesley raised his eyebrows. "Oh yeah?" he asked. Wesley and the congressman were classmates in school; he had followed the congressman's work closely ever since being elected to Congress. Somehow he couldn't see how the allegations against Edwards could be true.

For the next hour, the two men reviewed the final plans for the unveiling of their new product. Jase would postpone the final release until Wesley made contact with the UBC headquarters to discuss their concerns over the recent shakeup at the news studio. Other arrangements might be necessary if this continued to affect the station's audience.

Congressman Edwards walked down the corridor in the Rayburn House Office Building toward John Campbell's office. He had been trying to reach Nancy by phone since the previous evening after the allegations against him hit the news. He prayed that he could talk to Nancy before she heard the news from some other source, but each time he called, her telephone had either gone to voice mail or kept ringing. Even throughout the night when he called, there was no answer. Chris assumed that his wife had become overwhelmed by her work, or her phone had died. Now he entered Campbell's office and was greeted by his administrative assistant. "Go on in. He's expecting you," she directed Chris.

The older congressman looked up as Chris entered his office. Young Edwards looked as if he hadn't slept at all the night before. *"If I were in his shoes, I wouldn't have, either,"* Campbell thought to himself. The older congressman had seen too many scandals to count during his public service. He had been involved in a number of investigations. This morning, he dreaded talking with Edwards, whom he had come to look forward to meeting over lunch every Monday. There was a moment of awkward silence as the younger congressman sat down. He finally cleared his throat. "I'm pretty sure you've already heard what's been going around," he said to Campbell. "Apparently it's all over the hill; you wouldn't believe the stares I've gotten from the moment I got out of my car." Campbell smiled. "I can imagine." Chris looked directly at his counterpart. "I need you to know," he said resolutely, "I didn't do it." This was what Campbell expected him to say. But something was different. Rumors were already flying around that Chris Edwards may have become entangled in a political maneuver to damage the Constitution Party's election outcome; but there was no solid proof. His gut instinct told him that Chris just didn't have it in him to succumb to such temptation and... *"he's totally innocent,"* he thought to himself.

"Chris," the older congressman spoke quietly, "My better judgment tells me you're innocent. But," he hesitated, uncomfortable with what he had to tell his colleague. "It would be best for you to back away from any pending legislation, for the good of the party." There was stone silence for what seemed like minutes. The younger congressman had prepared himself for this response, but just hearing the words spoken was a stunning blow. It was a painful moment for Congressman Campbell, too.

158

He knew he had betrayed a trusted colleague, and equally as bad-compromised his personal principles. Chris turned to leave. "I'm so sorry it came to this," Congressman Campbell told his younger counterpart. Congressman Edwards nodded quietly, and left the office.

The administrative complex of Web-Connect, Inc. bustled with activity as the marketing team prepared to introduce the pending marketing campaign to the Board of Directors. Jase Childers, walked through the open door into Wesley's office without knocking. Their product that had been under development for nearly three years was nearing its release. If successful, it would be his first major success in this level of business. Crenshaw had indicated in a previous meeting that the next expansion of the company would give an opening for a vice president of marketing. He was the likely candidate for the position since Wesley had a personal practice of promoting from within the company. The CEO didn't look up when his marketing executive walked into the room. He was reading a letter quietly. Jase stood in front of his desk for a few moments, waiting patiently. He detected some tension in his superior's expression. Wesley looked up and handed the letter to Jase. "Take a look," he said with a sigh. The marketing manager took the letter and began reading:

"Dear Mr. Crenshaw,
        The National Association for Social
Equality exists to stand for the rights of minority
groups in America that have traditionally
been discriminated against. NASE publishes
an annual report of corporations who are
supportive of the alternative living
community. This report plays a major role
in the purchasing habits of the nation's citizens.

159

We recently spoke with your human resources
director to learn if your corporation had a policy
affirming the alternative living community,
and it does not.
　　　We would like to ask your written opinion
on adopting such a policy. I look forward to
your response.
Sincerely,
Darrell Youngblood,
President, NASE

Jase understood the implications of what he had just read. It could conceivably cause a loss of millions of dollars if the promotion failed. "Do we tell the directors?" he asked Wesley. They both knew that such an announcement would put their product's release on hold. "Not a word," Wesley responded. A sharp pain gripped his chest. Only yesterday, he was on the road to success. His personal creed was, "if you want something bad enough, you do what it takes to get it." He had lived by this creed religiously. No one could control his business, personal actions, or even thoughts. Now he was haunted by the recent meeting with his pastor. *"He was my trusted advisor, even if he didn't know it,"* Wesley lamented. *"Who can I go to now?"* The two men walked out into the hall together. His secretary informed them that the conference room was full, and the directors were ready to begin. Wesley tried to regain his usual confident composure as he walked toward the meeting room. On the outside he was the perfect picture of calmness; inwardly, he was tormented by an uncertain future.

　　　The conference room was full, with all twelve directors waiting around the large table. They began opening their folders in preparation for the meeting to begin when Wesley entered the room and sat down. The CEO laid his portfolio down, propped his elbows on the table, and rested his chin on his hands, clasped together. *"Do I cover this up, or should I tell them?"* he asked himself. The company's directors sensed that he might be about to share something unexpected. Wesley finally took a deep breath and began the meeting.

"Ladies and Gentlemen," he finally spoke up. "I just received a letter from one of the national advocacy organizations for the alternative lifestyle communities," he stopped and took a deep breath. "As each of us knows, the LGBT agenda has become a topic of increasing debate throughout the business and political world. Now, the National Association for Social Equality is demanding that we bow to their demands, or risk a national boycott of our product." One of the board members raised her hand, to speak. "What are their demands, and how could it affect this company?" she asked. "The letter is calling for the corporation to adopt a policy recognizing that we stand behind the LGBT community," Wesley responded. "And," he paused, feeling the weight of the circumstances. "If we refuse, there could be an all out war against our company. Any negative PR could cause our new product to lose millions of dollars."

"The room was silent. Wesley continued his talk. "Most of you know that our son came out of the closet several years ago," he said softly; so it will affect my family, either way we vote. But," he continued. I'm not one for being pushed around." Wesley again felt the same guilt that had come over him earlier that morning when he remembered how he had recently treated his pastor. "If I may voice my opinion," another board member spoke out. "I stand completely behind you. This corporation has worked hard to produce an excellent product, and we have the utmost confidence in your work. I say let's move ahead with the project." Almost spontaneously, each member raised their hand, nodding in agreement. "You're right," the first board member

161

concurred. "We can't allow a few bullies to change the way we do business."

Wesley was relieved. When he entered the conference room he had been tempted to keep this from his board. But he did the right thing, and left with a clear conscience, feeling rewarded, before his company's new release even hit the market.

Over 300 miles away, Nancy was exhausted from what seemed like a full day's work at the disaster site in Charleston. It was only noon, but she was stressed from the overwhelming load of coordinating between her staff, the emergency responders, and the volunteer teams. Before this week, she had encountered very little death in her life. The only time she had ever been present when someone died was when her father passed away two years earlier. Now, she had gone from shock, to indifference at the overwhelming number of lives that had been lost around her. The congressman's wife felt that she had to block all the images out so she could remain focused on her own work. She could fall apart after her work was completed. To compound her stress, she thought constantly about Chris' alleged harassment of his executive assistant. She had been plagued by this dilemma for two days now. Her worst fear was that it was true. Or was it that she may never know the truth? Nancy's cell-phone buzzed, alerting her of an incoming text. She reached in her pocketbook and pulled it out. The message on the screen read, "Call when you get a chance. I LOVE YOU!" It was from Chris. She felt like throwing the phone into the smoking rubble just twenty yards from where she stood, but gripped it tightly, fighting back the tears. *"Maybe, no one has noticed,"* she thought to herself.

Dr. Gambrell walked into the Southern Sirloin Steakhouse and spotted Gary Pace and Rick Hamby sitting toward the back of the dining area. The two board members had asked to meet for a follow-up of the recent board meeting. "Good afternoon, gentlemen," the college president greeted the two board members. They shook hands as he sat down at the table. Gambrell had always maintained a good working relationship with the board. As president of the university, he had a seat and voice on the board, but due to the last minute notification of the previous meeting, had not been able to call off an important obligation. So he had agreed to meet with these two to provide his personal thoughts on the matter. He wanted to share a positive report on the growth of the student body, and the spiritual renewal that was present throughout the campus. But the two board members were not engaged in his brief report of the campus life.

"I know you have a busy schedule," Gary changed the subject brusquely. "We just wanted to know what you think the outcome of the lawsuit will be." Dr. Gambrell was quick to respond. "In all honesty," he said, "I have no idea, if it goes to court. Whatever it may be, I will not compromise the integrity of this school." The two board members weren't as resolute in their own feelings about the matter. Rick took a deep breath. "That's just it," he interjected. "As good as things are going right now, I don't see how it could benefit the school to engage in a court fight. As a non-profit, finances are always tight." Dr. Gambrell wasn't convinced at the argument. "This isn't about money; it's an issue of principle," he countered. "I personally think that this is an attempt by the enemy to put his foot in our back door," he paused.

"But money *is* involved, and we can't deny that," Gary replied. "If we were to lose a civil rights suit, it could mean the loss of our tax exempt status. That would be devastating to the school's operation." Dr. Gambrell was a man of principle.

Although he was a soft-spoken person, he wouldn't back down when he felt like he was being backed into a corner. "I've spent my entire career as a Christian educator teaching my students to maintain strict loyalty to the Bible. Now is the time to teach them by my personal example; and I hope that you will stand behind me."

Gary leaned forward in his chair. "We're asking you to reconsider," he said. "This school has some standards that may have become outdated over the years, and in my opinion, too legalistic. Maybe we should revisit some of these policies." Dr. Gambrell could feel the pressure. *"Am I being told to compromise my Christian beliefs?"* he thought silently. "We teach our students to love sinners, as Christ loves them, but to hate the sin," he spoke up. "My job is to carry out the mission of the school as approved by the board, and what you're asking me is in complete violation of our policy." Dr. Gambrell held his ground. "Yes, and that can be changed," Gary challenged the university president. "Maybe I should just clarify that we're not trying to compromise our principles, but merely relax our standards." But Dr. Gambrell refused to waver; he made it clear that his position would remain the same, regardless of the outcome of any legal action.

11

Conflicting Emotions

The Trinity Christian Fellowship sanctuary was full on Sunday morning. Pastor Scott Crawford approached the pulpit with a heaviness he had never before experienced in his life. The previous days had produced several crises personally affecting him and his family, their small town, and the entire nation. While browsing online, Scott had seen the flood of comments by people from around the country who were in shock from the recent bombing in Charleston. Several throughout the community had come to him for comfort from their grief over losing a loved one in the catastrophe. The pastor was still dealing with his own personal emotions from his attack by Wesley Crenshaw. In spite of all these overwhelming circumstances, somehow Scott was able to make it through his morning sermon.

After closing the worship service with prayer, the pastor greeted each member personally as they left to go home. He was pleasantly surprised to see that Chris Edwards had slipped in during his morning sermon. Scott knew that Chris needed to talk; he paused from speaking to the Church members to arrange to meet the congressman at the Blue Ridge Café for lunch. The Church members finally filtered out, and Scott locked the door to the sanctuary before leaving with Connie.

When the pastor and his wife arrived at the Café, fortunately there wasn't a large crowd, and they were able to find a seat away from the few who were already eating. They exchanged casual greetings with Chris while waiting for their orders to arrive. After a few moments of silence the congressman spoke. "I'm sure you're aware of what's been going on in my life," he stopped for a moment. Both Scott and Connie had heard about the allegations against the congressman, but neither one believed any accusations. Edwards was a man of character. He was clearly caught up in a political battle to win the election; even if it called for the murder of his character. "This is a political maneuver," Scott told the congressman. "But I also believe it is a spiritual battle. These things happen to those who are willing to stand up to evil. No one in Congress has taken such a radical stand like this for years." Edwards nodded thoughtfully. "And the battle seems to get worse by the day," he agreed.

"How is the family dealing with all of this?" Connie asked him. "Nancy has been occupied by the disaster recovery operations in Charleston," the congressman explained. "I've tried to call her for several days. The only time we spoke was just for a few minutes, and it was very cold," he said with a heavy heart. "You need to go see her," the pastor encouraged his friend. "She's hurting, and vulnerable to all the rumors flying around her." Edwards knew he needed to go to Charleston; he should have already gone, but dreaded what might happen when he found his wife. Scott and Connie encouraged Chris to keep communicating with his family, and not back down from his resolution in Congress. The conversation finally changed, and they discussed the latest events in Blue Ridge Heights. The congressman was genuinely interested in the ongoing conflict

166

with the local school, and promised to talk with attorney Jeff Godwin about the matter again.

Harold Gentry sat in the control room during a commercial break between news segments. The news corporation still hadn't decided on a permanent replacement for Marvin Maddox, and was busy reviewing the prospective replacements' broadcast submissions. A new presidential election ad was just beginning. Senator Roger Francis appeared on the screen, walking through a park. He approached a swing with a small child and began pushing him. "Hi, I'm Roger Francis," the politician opened the political ad with a congenial smile on his face. "Do you want a President who will destroy your child's future? Or a leader that will take away the freedoms that we have taken for granted for centuries? This is what my opponent can do for you. He also stands behind friends who use their offices for their own personal pleasure. If you vote Progressive Party, I promise reform in Washington." The commercial ended. *"One more blow to Senator Smith,"* Harold thought to himself. With the Party's scandal involving Congressman Edwards, their strong stand on social equality issues, and their staunch opposition to abortion, this party would never win. *"But it will be a good fight,"* he thought to himself. *"That will pull the ratings back up for sure."*

Kelly Graham pulled into the parking lot of Godwin and Associates. After receiving a telephone call earlier this morning, she agreed to meet with Attorney Jeff Godwin to discuss his proposed strategy for having the anti-Christian literature banned from the school. When she entered the office, she was immediately escorted back to see Mr. Godwin. "I've been working with several others on these issues," Mr. Godwin told

167

her as he shook her hand. I think we have a good chance of having it overturned." His pleasant disposition had already put Kelly at ease. "You don't know how much this means to me-and the other parents," Kelly said appreciatively. "How can we keep this anti-Christian propaganda from being forced on our children?" The attorney looked up from the notes he had been writing on his pad.

"I think we can get a judge to issue an injunction," he informed his client. "This will at least keep this material away from your children until we can get a final court ruling." Mr. Godwin spent the next several minutes explaining the process to the PTA President. He agreed to keep her informed as the case developed. She left his office with a sense that perhaps, the issue would be over, soon.

Randall Smith sat in his office reviewing some notes for the upcoming debate. He looked up from his work when he heard a political commercial by his opponent, Roger Francis airing on the flat screen television on the wall. The senator sighed as he listened. This one accused him of having knowledge of Congressman Edwards' alleged harassment of his staff member; in so doing, implying that Smith was unfit for office. He had to make a decision. Most of the Constitution Party believed that Edwards' accusation was politically motivated to damage his resolution to the House floor; but no one was willing to stand behind him. Still, if Senator Smith chose to defend him it could wreck his chances of winning the presidency.

His thoughts were interrupted by the telephone ringing in the receptionist's office on the other side of his door. She was still out to lunch, so he picked up the receiver. "Randall Smith," he answered. It was Alivia Hollingsworth, his campaign manager on the other end. "I've been expecting you," he greeted her. She sounded rushed. "We need to discuss some changes before the debate," the campaign manager informed the senator. "What do you have in mind?" he asked her, curiously. "Some damage control," she responded. Senator Smith knew what she was referring to. "I just saw the advertisement. I was hoping this wouldn't get dirty," he sighed. "Well, he started it. My job is to make sure you can finish it in the debate," Alivia sounded as if she was about to step in a boxing ring herself. "If you're free this afternoon I'll come over to get you prepped." Smith knew she would try to encourage him to fight back, but he had already made up his mind. His was going to be a clean campaign. "I'm tied up this afternoon," he replied. "But stop by tomorrow after lunch and we'll make a plan."

It was a mild sunny afternoon in Princeton, West Virginia. The sky was a clear blue, contrasting against the dark green forested mountainside as Russell Taylor drove along the winding road leading to his house. But in spite of the beautiful day on the outside, the elderly minister felt a strong burden. His heart was heavy for Scott Crawford. He had continued to follow Scott's ministry developments, and shared his joys-and concerns for the community in which he ministered.

As Rev. Taylor drove around a wide curve on the outskirts of town, the old white Church where he pastored for nearly thirty years came into view. He slowed down and turned into the parking lot. As long as he could remember he had spent every Thursday afternoon at the Church in private prayer. That was his time that he spent alone with God, interceding for each of his Church members and praying for the Lord's presence to move his message on Sunday morning. Even after retiring, he had kept this habit. The older minister walked through the double doors between a small foyer and the sanctuary. Away from the city life, it was refreshing to live in a small community where one could go to the Church at any time and not be hindered by a locked door. The retired pastor walked slowly down the aisle and sat down on the front pew. He was no longer able to kneel at the altar because of his bad knees, but he could still pray. The heavy burden that had overwhelmed him all day began to fade as a spirit of intercession washed it away.

He prayed for Scott and his family who were facing a strong attack. Their faith was being tested, and he could feel the magnitude of their trial. And he prayed for Congressman Edwards. The retired minister hadn't met the lawmaker, but he felt as if he knew him from all that Scott had shared about him. And then he called David Gambrell's name, the president of King University. The issues that he was battling could very easily cripple the school. But the spiritual giant who was pleading for Dr. Gambrell to be strong and not waver, knew that the God he was crying out to was able to overcome this battle, too.

Back in Washington Reid Davis walked the distance from the Russell Senate Office Building over to the Rayburn House Office. Senator Francis had asked him to deliver a package to Jessica James. The young man walked into Congressman Edwards' office. Jessica was the only staff member remaining for the day and was shutting her computer down to leave. "I've been asked to deliver this to the congressman," he told her as he laid the manila envelope on her desk. Edwards' assistant avoided looking directly at him, but she thanked him as he turned to leave. *"Strange,"* Reid thought to himself as he went back into the long hallway.

The table had been cleared, and Connie began washing what was left of the dishes from the evening meal. Jordan and

Brianna were just leaving to go to the last high school baseball game of the season. It had been a good year for the Blue Ridge Heights Academy. If their team won this game, they would advance to the state playoffs. The two siblings were joining nearly all of the school to support their team's efforts. While eating supper Connie noticed Scott was unusually silent, but didn't say anything about it while the children were still in the room. She knew that her husband was under tremendous stress from the weight of the community and Church crises resting on his shoulders. And now his friend, Congressman Edwards had been caught up in a horrendous scandal that threatened to destroy his family, and perhaps change the outcome of the upcoming elections. When she turned around from the sink, Scott was still sitting quietly at the table. "What is it?" she asked, concerned about what was troubling her husband.

"I met with the board today," Scott replied. "Finances have been down for the last month, and now…" he trailed off. Scott didn't know which Church members contributed, nor how much. But he was certain that Wesley must have followed through with his threat to withdraw his support from the Church. Several of his close friends had not been present last week either. Scott knew of other Churches whose members had withheld their tithes in order to have their way in personal disagreements. He never thought that this would happen in his own small town Church. *"Most Churches our size can't support a paid office staff or a full time pastoral salary,"* he thought to himself. "The board has voted to eliminate your office position." Scott dreaded telling his wife, but Connie was already expecting to hear this. She walked over to where he sat and squeezed his hand. "We'll get through this," she assured him. "This isn't the first time we've faced a financial crisis."

Scott was always a strong and composed man; but in the face of the overwhelming pressure he was dealing with, he could see no way out." I'll have to find an outside job, or we're sunk," he said. He had held a bi-vocational job in an earlier pastorate, and was blessed to devote his full time to his present ministry. Scott was willing to find another job now, but didn't know how long it would take to find one, given the present state of the economy. The pastor remained quiet for the rest of the evening, trying to process the numerous crises that he, his family, Church and community had been thrown into. He felt the burden of everyone else's struggles; right now, he didn't have the strength to carry the load. Scott lay awake late into the night, still worrying about the sudden change of circumstances in his Church, and how his loss of salary might affect his family. He had a wife and two children to support. *I might even have to resign the Church,"* the painful thought rang through his mind before finally drifting off to sleep.

A cold atmosphere sat at the table in Congressman Edwards' home, too. He had stopped by for some Chinese carry-out for evening dinner on his way back from the Capitol. The congressman and his two sons ate in silence. As he agonized in silence, he noticed Jamie watching him eat. "How could you do this to mom?" he suddenly shouted, slamming his fists on the table before storming out of the room. "I-" Chris couldn't find the words to say to his son, and stopped in mid-sentence.

Justin remained seated. "Dad, I know it's not true," he spoke softly. The congressman knew his son's words were genuine. "Thank you, son," he tried to manage a smile. "I know this hasn't been easy on either of you." Justin stopped eating and put his fork down. "Everyone has been talking behind our backs at school. That's why Jamie is having such a hard time."

172

Edwards leaned forward in his chair. "What else have you heard?" he asked his son. "Well, someone said that you were being called out because of that resolution you're working on. It started making sense then." They both reflected in silence for a moment before the congressman's son spoke again. "So, why aren't you fighting it?" he asked. "You know," Chris said contemplatively. "I really thought about fighting back, but something told me just to lay it down." Justin shook his head. "And how is that going to help things?" he asked. "The truth is on our side; it will eventually come out," Edwards replied with a smile. Justin knew his father was a man of honor and true character. "I'm going to go watch the debate," the congressman said, standing up. "Do you care to join me?" Justin nodded, and followed his father into the living room.

Inside the Charlotte Civic Center, the two presidential candidates faced an audience of several thousand spectators who followed the questions carefully. Randall Smith felt the load of the numerous issues that could make, or break his chances of becoming the next president. He was ready to defend his party's platform. The conservative candidate had done extremely well in his response to several questions regarding the LGBT agenda. But he feared that his party's present scandal posed an even greater threat than his opposition to the same sex marriage issue.

Senator Smith," the moderator addressed the Constitution Party's candidate. "To this point, you have run what the public has perceived as a clean campaign. But the political world carries a constant flow of conflict. Where do you stand regarding the harassment allegations against Congressman Edwards?" The senator faced the camera confidently. "During my 25 years of service to this nation I've seen my share of controversy," he answered. "I've learned to be cautious when lending my endorsement because I've been let down too many times; but in this case, I would stake my campaign on Congressman Edwards. I know Mr. Edwards personally, and consider him to be a man of highest integrity." he said without hesitating. A hushed murmur went around the large auditorium as the audience either agreed with the Senator, or hoped his words would swing the debate in their candidate's favor.

When the audience got quiet, the moderator continued. "Mr. Francis," he addressed the Progressive Party's candidate. "You may respond to Mr. Smith's comments." Senator Francis faced the camera with a wide grin. "That's easy," he responded. "I will stake this campaign on Congressman Edwards' word as well!" A roar of laughter erupted from the audience, and the senator held up his hand with a more serious expression on his face. "I find it very disturbing that harassment among some of my congressional constituency has become the norm of society. While it is beyond my power to change the sad circumstances in Mr. Edwards' office today, when I am elected as your President, I will uphold a zero tolerance for harassment of any kind from our nation's leaders." The audience burst out in applause, and the moderator waited for the interruption to subside.

Behind the curtains, the senator's assistant was watching the debate from a large flat screen video monitor with several others from both of the presidential candidates' campaign staffs. Reid caught his breath. While he had suspected something unusual was going on for a long time, he just couldn't place his finger on it. But now he knew it was a set up. It all made sense. He couldn't prove it, but he knew this had occurred at least once more in the past. During the previous presidential election, one of the candidates for the Constitution Party had also been accused of making advances on his administrative assistant. Although Senator Francis was not in that race, Reid had been asked to

174

deliver a package to the young aide who had made her accusation. She suddenly resigned not long after that had happened, and the candidate dropped out of the race. Nothing further was said about the incident. Reid was supposed to be taking notes on the debate to provide critical input to Senator Francis; but he couldn't focus for the rest of the night as he struggled in his mind about what would be the right thing to do.

Wesley Crenshaw parked his car and walked toward the Trinity Christian Fellowship office. When he pulled on the door's handle it was locked. *"Something must be wrong,"* the businessman thought to himself. *"Someone is always in the office."* He peered through the glass door to look inside. The lights were out, and Connie's desk had been cleared off. *"What's going on?"* Wesley wondered. After an emotional week, he had taken the afternoon off to speak with the pastor. He was here to make some amends. As he turned to leave, Scott's car pulled into the parking lot and stopped. The pastor got out and greeted Wesley as he approached the office. "It's good to see you, Wesley," he shook his hand before unlocking the door. Pastor Scott turned on the light and the two walked inside. "Come on in." He invited his estranged Church member into his study.

Scott's emotions were whirling. As a pastor, he was expected to exemplify a Christ-like spirit, but right now he didn't feel very "pastorly," as he was often described by some of the older Church members. He was still battling his personal feelings from his last conversation with Wesley. Although the pastor tried to conceal these feelings, Wesley noticed a cynical expression on his face; even a sense of distance. The businessman knew he had been hard on his pastor. Now, he felt convicted because he had wrongfully heaped a heavy burden on

175

the minister. He was broken, and sat before his pastor without his usual air of confidence.

"I don't know how to begin," he fumbled for the right words. "Scott," he continued. "I came to ask for your forgiveness, but first I need to tell you why." The emotional barrier that had placed a wedge between the two began to melt away as the pastor listened to a totally different person than who had confronted him and his wife several weeks ago. "I recently received a letter informing me that the company is coming under attack from that civil rights organization," he paused. "Was this the Association for Social Equality?" Scott asked. "Yes, how did you know?" Wesley nodded. "I was introduced to their strong arm tactics by a mutual friend," the pastor continued. "David Gambrell, from King University." Wesley had already heard of the action that NASE had taken against the university; his attorney had told him just yesterday over lunch. "As I read that letter," Wesley continued to speak softly, "I realized that I had done the very same thing to you, and the Church." There was remorse in his voice. "It's easy to ignore our own faults," Scott told his Church member. "Sometimes the Lord uses crises in our lives to help us put our priorities back in order." Wesley knew his pastor was right; he was beginning to reorder his own priorities.

"So, have you spoken to your son?" Scott inquired. "To tell you the truth, we've spoken only once since he left," Wesley confessed. "Karen and I just don't know how to communicate with him." The businessman normally kept his personal life and feelings to himself. He didn't want to come over as being a man with any problems. But his pride had been stripped; today he spoke to Scott in humility. "How *do* I talk to him?" Wesley was almost begging for his pastor's counsel. "The most important

176

thing you can do is to show him your love," Scott encouraged him. "Not just as his parents, but as a Christian. One of the lies that the LGBT agenda propagates, is that if Christians don't accept this lifestyle, we're hate-mongers. This spreads confusion among many people like your son. But the Devil is the author of confusion," he explained. "It's okay not to condone his lifestyle. But we condemn the sin, not the one who is caught in sin." Wesley was still listening quietly. Scott counseled Wesley that, by showing unconditional love, he could win his son back faster; even if it didn't happen right away.

"But it's not that simple," the businessman insisted. "The LGBT agenda has a strong hold on those who identify with its community; you're right, it's a complex problem, but over time, you can win him back," the pastor continued to encourage him. "Don't just talk to him, but listen to what he has to say, and then respond accordingly. Give him gentle instruction, using the Bible to support your views, and then wait for the Holy Spirit to do His work," he urged Wesley. "The Bible tells us that faith comes by hearing the Word of God. We have to trust God to plant that seed of faith that he needs." All the time Scott was talking to Wesley he wondered if his words were being accepted. Wesley was drinking in every word. He had come, dreading meeting his pastor, but he had found healing. Now he could hardly wait for his family to find theirs.

The two men continued talking for nearly an hour. Wesley not only asked his pastor's forgiveness; he also pledged his full support in his church ministry. In spite of the threat that NASE was making to his company, Wesley vowed to respond to the advocacy organization with a firm position; while his company respected every individual as an important member of society, he would not bow to their desires and endorse their lifestyle. All employees would continue to be treated with respect, without any preferential treatment.

As they discussed his change of heart, Scott also wondered how Wesley and Karen would feel about the recent court action the PTA had brought against the School District. After all, part of it was in response to Karen's lessons in her classroom. His church member seemed to be reading his mind. "Karen just talked with the school district superintendent," he told his pastor. "And the irony about it is that when the subject came up, she didn't want to include our Christian beliefs because she wanted to avoid any conflict." The pastor nodded thoughtfully. "Maybe this can be a lesson for us all. As Christians, we're in God's army; as good soldiers for Christ, we must be willing to stand for our faith." Scott again felt that he was preaching to himself. The circumstances within their community and even around the nation were beginning to challenge the entire Church world. *"With so much persecution of the Christian faith overseas, would we be willing to stand for Christ if it ever comes to our own land?"* he wondered.

12

A Solemn Assembly

Both houses of Congress rested from session the day following the presidential debate. In spite of Senator Smith's strong performance, Roger Francis was proclaimed the winner by all major television networks. The members of the Constitution Party began to accept the fact that their candidate would not be winning the election unless something miraculous occurred.

Reid Davis entered the Rayburn House Office Building to deliver some notes from Senator Francis to several members of the Progressive Party. He passed the Speaker of the House's office. The young executive's heart was pounding. Earlier that morning when he was asked to make the run over to the House Office Building, the thought had crossed his mind that maybe he should go to the Speaker. Reid was torn between revealing what he knew, or just forgetting about a conspiracy that had destroyed a good man's marriage, professional life, and possibly even cost the country a good President. *"But what if I'm wrong?"* Davis wondered. He was well liked by the senator, and knew that with a recommendation from his office, he had the chances of a promising career in politics. On the other hand, if he shared his fears with the Speaker of the House, and Senator Francis was not guilty, it would destroy his future in Washington. Reid hesitated before entering the Speaker's office and then opened the door. If they believed him, they believed him; but if not, he could sleep with a clear conscience.

An atmosphere of unrest was growing at King University. Dr. Gambrell was noticeably quiet wherever he went. He was visibly stressed by the legal issues plaguing the school. When the news media picked up on the action being taken by the Department of Justice, rumors began spreading that the school was being forced to compromise its Christian beliefs. Some had speculated that the school had lost its tax exempt status, and Dr. Gambrell would be replaced by a new president in the upcoming school term.

The students sat in the auditorium for the Friday morning chapel service, and the room became quiet as Dr. Gambrell approached the podium. "This hour is usually devoted to a message meant to edify and encourage the student body," he addressed the student body. "But this morning, I would simply like to talk with you about what the school has been going through, and how we will respond to the community."

The president stepped out from behind the podium and walked to the edge of the stage where he could speak more informally to the students. "I'm aware of all the rumors that have been flying around," he continued. "I initially felt it was in the best interests of the school to keep it away from the student body; but when it begins to affect your academic and personal lives it's time to be transparent with you." He had the attention of the entire student body, who all wanted to know the truth behind this crisis that had become a national news item. "Unfortunately the conflict involves an alumnus that was living a lifestyle contrary to our beliefs as a Christian institution. In fact, a wave of anti-Christian sentiment has swept across the country over the last decade or so; now, a small minority of the population are attempting to force their own values on the Christian Church. This has forced us to re-think, and affirm our Christian values," Dr. Gambrell continued. "Two of our directors, Rick Hamby and Gary Pace, have resigned the board due to philosophical differences." The students listened with concern as their leader began to open up about everything that had transpired over the past weeks.

"Some very threatening legal action has been brought against the school," Dr. Gambrell informed the students. "It started with an organization called the National Association for Social Equality. Their desire is not just to have legalized in every state what they refer to as "same sex marriage," but also to force the Christian community to accept it within our ranks." He paused to take a breath. "We will not waver from our biblical stand," he stated resolutely. The student body burst into spontaneous applause, affirming their unity in the face of this conflict.

When the clapping subsided, Dr. Gambrell continued his talk. "I am sharing this, not to cause worry, but because each one of you can play an important part in affecting the outcome of this crisis." He lowered his voice for emphasis. "Here's what I would like to put before you. "First of all, we need to focus; focus on the reason you came here," he proposed. "Spend your time becoming grounded in the Bible, whether that is your college major, or not," he urged the students. "And I will refocus on my purpose as your professor and campus administrator. If we can regain sight of our purpose for the time, it will keep us on the right track." Dr. Gambrell looked around the auditorium at the thousands of students as they listened to his plea.

"And secondly, next week King University will be hosting a national pastor's conference right here on this campus. Some of these pastors are already engaged in similar battles within their own Churches. Others will be forced to face the same issues in the near future. And so, I'm asking for your united prayers for this conference. Pray for the pastors to leave renewed and resolved to stand firm no matter what they may have to face. And let us pray for revivals throughout the Church community. If our Churches are revived, our nation will be restored." Dr. Gambrell turned and walked quietly back behind the podium on the stage. He leaned over the podium in silence for a moment before closing the chapel service in prayer. The only sound that could be heard was the still hissing of the cool air coming from a large round air vent mounted high above the floor in the ceiling.

The general manager of UBC Headquarters sat in his office preparing for a long day. He had a decision to make; no, he had already made his decision, but carrying it out would be difficult. The network ratings had plummeted since Marvin Maddox left the news agency. Marvin's delivery style, though not in alignment with the more liberal philosophy of most of his associates, had brought a fresh perspective to the news industry. And the high ratings that UBC News had consistently maintained during his tenure as anchorman validated that his pure news delivery was accepted around the country. If something didn't change before the next ratings report was released, they were sure to lose some major program sponsors.

Mike walked down the hall to the conference room where he had asked Harold Gentry to meet with him. The news director was already waiting when he walked through the door and sat down. There was no easy way to terminate an employee, so the best thing to do was go ahead and get it over with. "I just don't think this is going to work," he said, looking directly into his news director's eyes. "I'm not following you," Gentry responded, puzzled. "I mean," Mike said slowly, "Our numbers were soaring. Our news anchor walked out for *who* knows why, and now the ratings are lower than the U.S. economy," he spoke sharply. "Oh, that happens every time there's a change-out in the news industry," Harold tried to cut in. He saw where this meeting was leading. "Yes, but there's more," Mike continued. "Nearly every member of the production team has told me that you're relationship with Maddox was very hostile, and several even used the word, 'harassing.'" Harold's hands were clasped tightly together in front of his face nervously, with his elbows on the table. "I have repeatedly asked you to change up the programming, but you still haven't complied," the station manager continued.

"What's gotten into you? I'm only directing the staff the way you've always asked me to," Harold fired back at his manager. "Yes, but things change, and so have I," Mike didn't hesitate to answer the challenge. "I just don't think our listeners want to hear the biased reporting that this industry has come to embrace over the years, and I have the numbers to prove it." He decided to give Harold one more opportunity, and spoke calmly. "I'll give you a few days to think it over. If you don't think you can conform, then I'll accept your resignation." Harold stood up abruptly. "You'll lose your ratings, and money," he snapped. "So, is that your answer?" Mike asked the news director. Harold stormed out of the room. The manager glanced at his watch. It was only 11 AM. He still had time to call Marvin Maddox.

The past week had been an emotional roller coaster for Congressman Edwards. After risking his office to introduce his resolution, it had won much support, only to have it-and his family destroyed by a hostile political tactic. Initially, he didn't know why the senseless accusations were made against him. Now, the truth had been told by a brave aide whose conscience wouldn't allow him see a good man wrongfully ruined. Early that morning he received a call from A.J. Wilson, who told him of Reid Davis' visit to his office. He was elated. The truth had come out. As Chris walked into the cafeteria of the House Office Building, he saw the group of his close constituents sitting at their usual table. Congressman Wilson stood up to greet Edwards as he approached the table. The Speaker was relieved that the truth was now known; he was ashamed that his party had doubted Congressman Edwards' integrity.

John Campbell and Chaplain Peter Cartwright also sat at the table. While failures and conflict among the lawmakers was almost a constant, the chaplain felt it his calling to be there for emotional and spiritual support for each of these men who he considered to be his flock. Upon learning of the accusations against Campbell the first thought that came to his mind was of the story of David in the Bible, when he was being hunted down by King Saul. He reminded the congressman that throughout the entire conflict with the king, David "behaved himself wisely in all that he did," both in good times and the bad. [30]   The chaplain believed Congressman Edwards had exhibited the same character through his own ordeal.

"I want to be the first to offer my apology for not standing up for you," Congressman Campbell expressed to Edwards with sincerity. "You're a man of upstanding character. No one would even consider a resolution such as yours if their heart wasn't in the right place," he said. The others at the table agreed with him wholeheartedly. "You're feelings were only human," Edwards replied graciously. "No hard feelings. Now, I need to know if you're still with me on the Freedom bill?" The congressmen all nodded. "We should be asking if you still stand with us," Campbell spoke up. "As soon as this news hits the press, the American people will see you for who you truly are. That's the kind of leader they want, and it's who we need to be as well," Campbell spoke again. "I understand that you have a staff opening?" he quipped. "I do," Chris responded with a smile. "If you know of any good prospects, send them my way." He stood to leave. "Gentlemen, I hate to leave good company, but I have a flight to catch," he waved to them as he left the table.

The King University board of directors had just convened another special meeting in response to the ongoing battle between the school and NASE. The atmosphere was tense. Each member understood that today's vote would commence possible legal action from the Department of Justice. NASE was reportedly preparing to bring Civil Rights charges against the school for alleged discrimination in their policies for accepting students and even the hiring of faculty and staff. The latest charge was of grave concern to each of the members; it was their Christian conviction that no individual who did not profess a Christian testimony, and believe that the Holy Bible was the Christian's standard for living, would be considered for employment at the school. After all, how could the school promise a Christian education to its students who had come for that purpose, if their teachers didn't have a Christian testimony themselves? Now, the threat had become a very real possibility. [31]

"We note that the minutes will reflect that members Gary Pate and Rick Hamby have tendered their resignations to the board," Jesse Wood stated as he opened the meeting. That was the only thing said about the two former board members being absent. "We asked you to begin prayerful consideration for nominating members to fill these vacancies," the board chairman continued. "We will receive any nominations you may have, but would first like to hear a report from Dr. Gambrell on the present state of the student body." He nodded to David Gambrell who was sitting at the opposite end of the conference table.

"First, I want to express how much we appreciate your faithfulness throughout this ordeal," Dr. Gambrell rose to speak. "Not many people realize the tremendous burden that you as our directors always carry, especially during conflicting moments such as what you're dealing with now." The board members' response to the president's sentiments was much more receptive than the two former members who had asked him to meet over dinner. "Since our last meeting, I devoted a full chapel service to address any questions about our position on the moral stand that we have taken. I asked the student body to recommit themselves to the spiritual integrity of the university, and to hold you, our leaders in their daily prayers. Since that day, I have sensed a genuine renewal among our students, both in their academic focus, as well as their spiritual lives." The board members accepted Dr. Gambrell's report with a round of applause as he returned to his seat. They were touched by the unity that was emerging among the students and faculty while the legal action still stood over the school.

Attorney Jeff Godwin and Kelly Graham left the Greenville County Circuit Court, jubilant over the judge's ruling. After a brief hearing, he granted an injunction prohibiting the anti-Christian literature from being distributed in schools throughout the entire State. As opposed to an annual distribution of New Testaments to elementary school students, the book was an open attack against the religious beliefs of Christian students. To allow its distribution would be an endorsement of its hostility by the State. Jeff explained that this ruling was temporary, but it would give them time to prepare a strong case to bring against the organization. He promised to keep her informed on the case's progress.

"Good evening, ladies and gentlemen," Marvin Maddox opened the evening news broadcast. "For the last several months, the presidential campaign has progressively gotten more competitive. Just a few weeks back it seemed that the Progressive Party was headed for a certain victory in the upcoming general elections," the anchorman spoke as if he had not been absent from his job. "But there are rumors that a major upset could be on the horizon for the Progressive Party," he continued. "We will follow these developments and bring you more news as soon as we have heard more on the subject."

"In other news," he continued, "the National Association for Social Equality faces an uphill battle as it prepares for a showdown with King University in Charlotte, North Carolina. The conservative Christian university has faced other battles throughout its more than one hundred year history. This could be the one to define its legacy. Alumni and other Christian organizations throughout America have pledged their support for the institution. But," the anchorman paused for a breath," NASE isn't going down without a fight. A million man march is being planned at the US Capitol to try to sway the upcoming Senate vote on H.R. 291, the bill sponsored by Congresswoman Sara Jackson. This has become a fight for principle; a struggle that could thrust the liberal agenda ahead, or the start of a national revival of our country's traditional moral values."

The station manager turned away from the observation window with a sense of satisfaction. There was no hint of slanted reporting. This was the kind of journalism he once knew; it was the kind of journalism his station would promote. In spite of losing his news director, a highly qualified professional, he had done the right thing.

The sun was getting lower over Charleston, South Carolina. The sky had been a smoky gray for over a week after the bombing at the stadium; ash fell on cars across the city throughout the week. Now the air was clear, and the sky was blue with only a hint of smoke from the site of the recent terrorist attack. Nancy completed her responsibilities at the disaster site before five o'clock, and then went to her room to freshen up before getting some dinner. Exhausted from the stressful activities over the week, she laid down on her bed to rest for a few minutes, and fell asleep. It was nearly dark when she woke up, but she went on downstairs to the restaurant lounge on the first floor for a late supper. The booth in the corner of the restaurant where she normally had her meals was already taken, so the young woman took a seat on one of the high stools at a cocktail table in the opposite corner.

Several local patrons sitting nearby recognized her when she entered the room. "Pity the poor woman," an older woman said, "but I can't say that I blame her for leaving the cheater," she presumed. "I heard that she left two boys behind," another one sitting across from her said. "If it's true, I'd say she's worse than her husband." The small group of women who met regularly each week for a card game wasn't aware that she could hear what they were saying. But her mind was hundreds of miles away.

Nancy was jolted back to reality by the sound of the national news breaking in on the program that was playing on the large flat screen televisions mounted throughout the restaurant.

188

The words *NEWS BULLETIN* flashed across the screen and Marvin Maddox began speaking.

"Good evening. We are interrupting the regularly scheduled program to bring some new developments in the presidential race," he announced. "Some recent revelations have surfaced that could change the destiny of the upcoming election." The patrons throughout the dining area had stopped eating and were focused on the report. "This morning an executive assistant for presidential candidate Roger Francis came forward with allegations that put Senator Francis' work under close scrutiny. A subsequent investigation revealed that the Progressive Party's presidential candidate paid Chris Edwards' executive assistant, Jessica James, to bring claims of harassment against the congressman. This was intended to throw public opinion in favor of the Progressive Party which should have then, given them the presidency." Nancy's mouth fell open and tears began streaming down her face as she listened to the revelation of her husband's innocence. *"How could I have doubted?"* she asked herself. As distant as she had been from her husband, she wanted to believe that it was all just a mistake. Now he had been exonerated.

Chris Edwards pulled into the parking lot at the Charleston Grand Hotel, where Nancy was staying. He had called the front desk as he came into town to get her room number, hoping to surprise her. The door was locked when he reached her room, so he walked down to the lobby. "Has Nancy Edwards arrived back at the hotel?" he asked. The clerk pointed toward the restaurant lounge, across the lobby. "She went that way earlier," she informed him.

The congressman walked into the restaurant. He scanned over the seating area packed with patrons. Nancy was sitting in the far corner of the room watching the television. In the excitement of seeing his wife, he didn't notice that everyone was watching a news bulletin telling of his exoneration. But they recognized the public figure as he made his way toward Nancy.

The congressman's wife turned toward him as she saw his figure approaching her out of the corner of her eye. When she realized it was Chris, she jumped from the bar stool she was sitting on, knocking it over in her haste to get to her husband. All feelings of anger and doubt melted the instant her eyes met his. It was just as if it had been a terrible nightmare. She grabbed Chris and held him tightly, with tears still rolling down her cheeks.

Several of the guests were working at the disaster site and had come to know Nancy as she worked with the volunteer disaster teams. Having been in close contact with the congresswoman's wife, they were aware of the stress she was under. They shared Nancy's joy as she realized these claims were fabricated and her husband had been faithful to her.

There was no one sitting in the section where Nancy's table was located, and the couple made their way back to her seat to reunite with her husband while she finished her meal. "So, how about the boys?" Nancy asked. She had spoken with them twice since leaving for the emergency site, and sensed a distance between them. "Things have been pretty tense," Chris confessed. "They were with me when the news broke. But Jamie is still having a struggle with it." The reality weighed heavily upon the congressman that the pitfalls of his job had affected his sons so negatively. "I think it's pretty mopped up on my end," Nancy commented. "I'll be home this weekend, so we can all have a family sit-down and get things back together."

Chris stood up and pushed his chair in. "I have something that can't wait," he said to his wife. "Let's take a walk." The

190

congressman went to pay the bill while Nancy got her bag. When they went outside, he pointed down the sidewalk lined with giant oak trees, leading to the Charleston Battery, a long concrete walk overlooking the bay. As they walked slowly taking in the scenery, the two discussed the recent test of their relationship; how it all started, why it had taken so long to be reunited, and... Nancy suddenly stopped, turned to Chris and took his hands. "As difficult as this has been for me, I know it has been much harder for you," she said, looking into his eyes. "We both knew how dirty Washington can be. But I just wasn't prepared for this." Chris started to say something, but she gently put her finger over his lips. "I just want you to know that no matter whatever happens in the future, I'll never doubt you again." Chris wrapped his arms around her and held her close. The congressman had prayed for his marriage to be restored; now they walked in silence, hand in hand down the walkway under the full moon.

The U.S. Capitol was in an uproar. The revelation of Senator Francis' attempt to throw the elections was unprecedented. Never before had a presidential candidate been disqualified due to official misconduct. With just a few months to go before general elections, both parties were scrambling to study the procedure for securing a candidate to replace Senator Francis' nomination. Normal protocol for a vacancy called for the candidate who came in second place in the primary elections to assume the candidacy. But some were demanding for a replacement candidate to be named by Congress.

This uproar was the least of Senator Roger Francis' worries. He knew that an investigation would be started soon; he needed to talk with his attorney soon. When he stopped by the National Campaign Headquarters the next morning, not one

191

volunteer was present, and there was dead silence throughout the open office area. Amber Weaver, Francis' campaign manager looked up from her desk when she heard the senator coming through the front door. She picked up a sealed envelope and walked out to speak to him. "I am so glad to see you," Francis exclaimed when she entered the main office area. His usual confidence had been replaced with uncertainty. "Call Thomas Wainwright," he said, tersely. Amber faced the senator. "When I agreed to run this campaign," she spoke quietly, "I never bargained for this. I'm sorry, but I'm out. Here's my resignation." She put the envelope in Senator Francis' hand. Without a further word, she shouldered her purse and walked out the door.

Stunned, the senator sat on a table and pulled out his cell phone. He had to talk with Thomas. His publicist was known as the spin-doctor of politics. *"He can fix this,"* Francis thought. He took a deep breath and then dialed the number. "Thomas," the senator said anxiously when the publicist answered. "I need to see you as soon as possible." he asked with a shaky voice. There was silence on the other end, and the publicist finally answered. "Listen, I said to create a diversion, not start a constitutional crisis," he said sharply. Thomas had stayed up late taking in as much of the news as he could gather. His better judgment told him to get as far away from this controversy as quickly as possible. "I'm sorry, but I just can't risk representing this campaign any longer." The senator was desperate. Without support from his publicist his chances for the presidency were over. "Let's just talk about it," he pleaded with Thomas. "I can't fix this," Wainwright replied firmly. "The best thing you can do for yourself, and for your party," he hesitated, "is to hang it up." The senator touched the end call button on his phone and put it back in his pocket. He knew that it was over.

The students of King University had worked throughout the entire week to make sure everything was prepared for the annual pastor's conference, from mowing the lawns, to covering every detail of the buildings. In spite of the pending legal action against the school, students and faculty alike were convinced that a miracle would save the school from any harm that NASE might try to inflict. After recommitting themselves to their academic and spiritual life, the entire student body had regrouped with a new sense of unity.

Now, the campus overflowed with pastors from all over the United States. Pastor Scott Crawford and Russell Taylor were both featured speakers at the event. In the last seminar, Scott shared both his own and Congressman Edwards' testimony; how the congressman had been challenged by his epiphany, *"What if our nation's leaders were to return to the moral principles it was founded on?"*

After telling about the controversy that had erupted within Congress and the false allegations against Congressman Edwards, the young pastor said, "This morning I'd like to ask you, "What would happen if the *Church* assumed its proper place in society?" He paused long enough to allow his statement to sink in. "I believe that a mere one or two Christians sold out to the authority of God's Word, have more power to change our present national circumstances than all of Congress." He indicated that the floor was open for individual input. "It would certainly stir up some opposition," a pastor sitting near the front of the auditorium spoke out. This led to a very engaged discussion by several other members of the conference.

Another visitor stood up to address the audience. "About this 'million man march' that liberal organization is planning for next week, we have a big enough group here to have a counter-protest." A murmur went around the large audience. Rev.

Russell Taylor stood up and slowly moved with the aid of a walking cane, to the front podium. The room became quiet as he turned to face the audience.

"The consensus of this meeting is that there is a need for change in our nation, and Church," the older minister spoke out. "But I think we're missing out on something," he continued. "Protesting has its place in our society, and we must have Christians who are active in the political world," he leaned on the podium for support. "But we as God's servants have a more effective tool than these protesters." Scott felt a chill run down his arms and through his back as he listened to his mentor exhort the assembly. It was refreshing to sit and drink in the words of another minister for a change.

"I hear so many preachers saying that theirs is a "New Testament Church," Rev. Taylor continued. "But there's not very much going on in many Churches today that even resembles how the New Testament Church operated. Before they made any important decision, they prayed." The retired pastor had the attention of every person present. "And when they faced adversity-when Paul and Silas were thrown in prison for their Christian faith, they prayed. God miraculously opened the doors to their prison, and they were set free. [32] This same kind of praying could restore our freedom in America today; most importantly, the *spiritual* freedom the Christian Church has surrendered to this ungodly society." An overwhelming sense of God's presence was felt all around the auditorium. Some openly responded with "Amens." Others listened silently, but still drank in the beautiful spirit of unity that was present.

"Prayer must be the Christian's weapon of choice, and here's what I propose," Rev. Taylor continued to address the audience. "For the next seven days before Congress votes, I challenge you to go back to your Churches, and call God's people to a time of silent prayer. This wicked nation is standing in a balance. We will either continue to crumble, or the Church could lead this land back to a nation of peace and stability; prosperity, and right living. That's the only thing that can save America." The old preacher suddenly stopped speaking and his knees nearly buckled. Scott and Dr. Gambrell quickly assisted him to a chair.

Men and women alike began weeping throughout the audience. A spirit of reverence and brokenness flooded the auditorium. Before Rev. Taylor had started speaking, many of the audience had grown restless as the lunch hour neared. But now, the entire assembly had forgotten about the break as a supernatural anointing swept over the assembly. Like the disciples who were with Jesus on the mountain when he was transfigured, no one wanted to leave. [33]

After nearly a month of scrambling between meetings with the National Security Council and the National Incident Command Post at the site of the Charleston bombing, Aaron Crosby was beginning to feel better about the overall safety of the U.S. population. Between these meetings and his morning briefings to the President, the national security advisor had developed a list of proposed measures for the United States to adopt in response to the recent terrorist attack. No official terrorist organization had taken credit for the mass bombing, but intelligence officials were sure that it was the working of an organization they had been watching for some time. This morning, as Aaron presented his briefing in the Oval Office, the President didn't seem as concerned about the domestic safety measures that the adviser had prepared for his consideration. Interestingly, he wanted to talk about Israel and her mid-east enemies.

"There is reason for significant concern regarding the state of Iran and Israel," Crosby answered the President's request. "Where do you see the greatest threat?" President Duncan inquired. "The latest intel indicates that Iran could have enough enriched uranium to build a bomb within months," the President's adviser informed him soberly. "So what do you suggest?" President Duncan asked Aaron. He struggled for the right words. There seemed to be a genuine softness with the President as they discussed the crisis. "Now is the time to show some world leadership," Crosby suggested. "Send a message that we will stand behind Israel with no reservations, and then stand behind your words." The President's adviser continued to discuss their best options for a response to the threats against Israel. He knew that although he and the President had not seen eye to eye on every issue, his words were being considered carefully.

The meeting was concluded, and after Aaron left the office, President Duncan sat at his desk contemplating what should be done regarding this latest threat against their ally. He couldn't help but remember Aaron's previous admonition that America was under a curse because of their policy toward Israel. What if he was right? Congress had been requesting severe diplomatic and economic sanctions against Iran, who were becoming increasingly aggressive in their world policy. Now they were openly threatening the autonomy of Israel. *"It's time to take a stand,"* the President pondered quietly.

Over a mile away from the White House, the House of Representatives had just convened for its afternoon session. The Lower House had spent the morning listening to some miscellaneous speeches, and in final deliberations for both the H.R. 291 and the Heritage and Freedom Amendments bill. Both measures would be voted on shortly. H.R. 291 would be voted on first, and the Speaker of the House entertained the last speeches for and against the measure before the vote was cast. After the bill's sponsor, Sara Jackson, completed her last plea to pass the resolution, Congressman John Campbell was recognized to speak.

"To my esteemed colleagues," Campbell addressed the body of Congress, "I would like to speak to just one point against the passing of H.R. 291. Over the last several decades, our nation has become more and more anti-Christian in its public policy, and I regretfully concede that much of it has been propagated by this House." He paused to clear his throat. "No, I'm not arguing the virtues of Church and State," the congressman continued. "But we must recognize that this anti-Christian resolution, if endorsed by Congress would violate the national sentiment for a separation of Church and State. It may have begun in the 1960s when one woman pushed to have Bible readings removed from the public schools. Since that time, our nation has progressively become a more corrupt, violent and immoral society," he argued. "This bill before you will not only restrict the free worship of Christians in America. It will be one more nail in the coffin of all the freedoms that we as Americans hold so dearly. In all my years as a congressman, I have never witnessed any proposed law more despicable than this one that lays before us today. It only took one person to start this nation's decline; and it can stop right here with your vote, today. I urge my fellow lawmakers to do the right thing and reject the passage of this resolution." The congressman nodded in appreciation for his allotted time, and then returned to his seat.

Outside the Capitol a group of several hundred protesters were gathered, carrying signs and walking up and down the street. The large crowd that NASE had called for didn't come out. The interest of their smaller groups around the country had vanished over the last week. The Capitol police was prepared for the worst, with auxiliary officers on call, just in case the crowd became too large for the normal patrol to handle. But by mid afternoon it was probable that the crowd would dissipate before the final voting was cast.

Reid Davis had just accepted Congressman Edwards' offer to become his new executive assistant. The young aide was thankful he had risked his job as Senator Francis' assistant by sharing his suspicions to the House Speaker. He already felt that his new assignment was where he should be. Reid had been asked to attend the rally outside the Capitol and report to Edwards if there were any notable developments, or after it ended. *"It looks as if it's going to be a long day,"* he thought to himself, standing away from the small group of protesters.

Ten, nine, eight...the large red clock in the UBC Studio began counting backwards. Marvin Maddox looked into the camera as it completed counting down to zero and the ON AIR sign flashed.

"Good evening, and welcome to the UBC Evening News," he routinely opened the evening broadcast. "Tonight we begin with news of historical proportions breaking from the U.S. Capitol. Several months ago we began reporting on two resolutions in the House of Representatives in direct opposition to each other; one was considered by many to be a threat to the religious liberties of the nation. This first bill, House Resolution 291 was overwhelmingly voted down this afternoon by a margin of 400 to 35. Had it passed and gone through the Senate, this bill would have severely restricted the freedom of expression and religious practices of Churches and Christian organizations all over America. It would have inevitably opened the door to more government intrusion on individual religious liberties as well."

"Ironically, the *Heritage and Freedom Amendments Act* was passed by nearly the same margin of 396 to 39 votes. Critics are saying that it is merely an attempt to push Christianity through the back door of public life. However," he continued, "it carries some strong guidelines that not many people can argue against. The bill that was sponsored by Congressman Christopher Edwards and several other Constitutional Party members requires Congress to pass a balanced budget that will reduce spending by one percent each year until the deficit is gone. The bill also limits congressional terms from both houses to two consecutive terms, but one may be eligible for office again after sitting out one full term. One of the most notable points of this law is that it will reign in the power of the Supreme Court. The last proposed amendment will limit the time that any justice may serve to one ten-year term. But here's the kicker; legislators will be allowed to approve-or disprove all future laws on the merits of how well they align with the moral principles that were embraced by the founding fathers of America."

Mike Blackwell sat in the control room watching the communications analyst's computer screen. This technician was monitoring the station's evening Twitter feed. The station manager noted that since the evening broadcast began, the number of tweets had spiked tremendously into the thousands. A closer glance at the screen showed the vast majority of comments were in favor of the *Heritage and Freedom Amendments Act* that had just been announced.

Chris Edwards got out of his car and locked the door before walking toward Independence Towers. When he entered the lobby the security guard was watching a commercial on flat screen television mounted to the wall. "I've been listening to the report about your bill passing today," he told Edwards. "Yes, we've been working toward this day for months," the congressman replied with a broad smile on his face. Chris remained in the lobby talking about the bill with the guard. When the broadcast came back on the screen they paused to listen in.

"And finally this evening," the anchorman started his final segment. "There is another promising ending to the Civil Rights action brought against King University by the DOJ. You may remember that the National Association for Social Equality threatened action against this school if they did not change their policy to favor the alternative living communities. As NASE was preparing their star witness, Marcus Jefferson, an alumnus of King, to testify in the upcoming lawsuit, Jefferson suddenly withdrew his complaint and refused to testify against the school. Without this key witness, or any other testimony, the legs have been knocked out from under the case against the school."

"I don't know about you," Maddox concluded his broadcast, "but there seems to be a wave of refreshing reports from around the nation. This leads us to wonder, what is going on in America?" I'll let you think on that one tonight, and hope to see you again for the next broadcast of the UBC Evening News. Good night!" The cameras zoomed away from the anchor's desk as the closing credits began to roll.

13

A Glimmer of Hope

The George Washington Grand Hotel in the U.S. Capitol bustled with activity on Friday evening. A group of congressmen and their wives sat around a large table in its cafe for evening dinner. Chris and Nancy Edwards were running late, and arrived just as the group was beginning their meal. They sat down across from Senator William and Rebecca Hudson. John Campbell and A.J. Wilson were also in the group. Congressman Campbell was widowed, and Wilson's wife was unable to attend.

"We were beginning to think you had started on a new resolution and couldn't join us," Senator Hudson quipped as they sat down. Everyone laughed at the joke, but they knew there was some truth in it. Edwards was a passion-driven man. He had come to Washington to represent the people well; his actions had proven it, and those around him knew that he couldn't sit idle. The men began to discuss the latest development in the presidential race as Nancy and Rebecca struck up a conversation of their own.

Over the last months, Nancy had developed a strong bond with Rebecca. Their friendship was helping her adjust to the bustle of the fast-paced environment in Washington. "There's a big difference in you since we talked last week," Rebecca told her. "I was still coming out of shock from what Chris and I had gone through," Nancy agreed. "And the disaster recovery in Charleston was still on my mind." Rebecca was interested and genuinely concerned. "What's the latest on that?" she enquired. The news was still covering the cleanup of the bombing site, but not as often. "My personal involvement is over," Nancy told her friend. "Most of the recovery efforts are over and the local law enforcement are supervising the remaining cleanup. And Homeland Security will remain on site for another two weeks." The congressman's wife was relieved to be away from the carnage and destruction. Her continued presence around so much death had taken a clear toll on her, and it would be a long time before she could heal emotionally. The memory would always remain, but she would never regret her service to her country.

The remainder of the evening passed by for the entire group; everyone left, with no burdens remaining over the numerous crises that each of the lawmakers had been so heavily invested in. But they knew that the nature of their work could demand more sacrifices in the future. Congressman Campbell was leaving his office in three months. This was a result of the term limits their bill had placed on both Houses of Congress. But he was leaving knowing that he had played a major part in paving the road for the future success of his fellow congressmen.

Connie Crawford and Ruby Taylor sat at the kitchen table at the Crawford family residence. Both Scott and Connie were delighted to have the elderly minister and his wife drive all the way from Princeton for a weekend visit. While they were visiting, Russell Taylor was to bring the Sunday morning message at Trinity Christian Fellowship. Connie had many fond memories from her teen years, when Russell was the pastor of her

Church. The pastor's house was the place where the Church youth congregated every weekend. Now, Connie and Ruby talked about these memories, while she hosted her former pastor and his wife in her own house.

Scott and Russell sat in the living room talking over a cup of coffee. A special news report of the President's address to the nation from the White House was expected to begin at any time. The television was muted so they could talk while waiting for it to begin. Although the two ministers had communicated almost weekly by telephone, it was good to finally be together in person. Tonight, they conversed on the recent turn of events related to the school controversy in Blue Ridge Heights, and then, on the national level, with Congressman Edwards' dedicated work finally reaping some positive results.

Scott raised the volume when the special report prompt flashed across the television screen. The camera zoomed in on Marvin Maddox sitting behind the anchor's desk at the UBC Studio. "We interrupt your regularly scheduled broadcast as we await the President's address to begin at any moment," he informed his television audience. "While we wait, we will interview several key members of both political parties about what to expect from the President's address."

Inside the Oval Office, the camera man adjusted the focus on his video camera and turned on the lights in preparation for the President's speech. A knock came at the door, and a secret service agent opened it to screen the caller. Aaron Crosby was allowed to enter a moment later. President Duncan stood up from his desk to greet his national security adviser.

"Come in, Aaron," President Duncan shook his adviser's hand. "I still have a few minutes left," he said, appearing very relaxed even though his address would begin shortly. "I've wanted to thank you for reminding me about what is truly important," the President spoke freely. "I mean, I've come to realize that you were right about our relationship with Israel." Aaron's mind raced over all of the tension that had transpired between the two of them over the past several weeks. Now, President Duncan's temperament reflected a total turn-around. The President's adviser was astonished yet refreshed, by his sudden softness. "So, what caused you to change your mind?" he asked. President Duncan took a deep breath, reflecting. "I tell you what; let's meet for lunch tomorrow and I'll tell you about it." Aaron was hoping for a few more minutes with the President, but the broadcast supervisor motioned that it was time to begin the speech; the two shook hands as Aaron left the room.

The picture on the television screen in the Crawford's living room switched to the Oval Office. Scott Crawford and Rev. Taylor both leaned forward, anticipating what the President would say.

"Good evening, fellow citizens," President Duncan opened his address. "Tonight I would like to update you on where we stand as a nation both at home, and in the international community. For too long, we have been entangled with unnecessary gridlock in Washington. We have ignored the concerns of our own people, while catering to too many special interest groups, just for the sake of being re-elected; and all the while neglecting the things we were already elected to do." The President glanced at his notes as he continued.

"While I would like to place the blame on Congress-especially the Constitution Party," he grinned, "I can only put the blame on myself, as your leader. President Truman kept a sign on this very desk that said, 'The Buck Stops Here.' This has not been the case over the past several years, but from this day on, it will." The camera zoomed out from the close-up shot on the President, showing a wide view of the Oval Office.

"In an unusual turn of events over the past several months, Congress has joined together in an act of harmony I have never seen since I took office. Some time ago I learned that a grassroots movement to return the United States to its historical moral values had been started by a small group of congressmen. And this movement spread to a small Church in South Carolina, who began to pray. I don't think this desire was by some chance. It had to have come from a higher power," he spoke with conviction. "As much as I didn't want to admit this, some of the crises that we now face are a result of the ungodly values that have come out of Washington. Several of these we now face are so serious that I cannot handle them alone, and Congress is even helpless to deal with the most severe. If it is to survive, our country must have the help of God. So I have re-committed myself to do the work I was elected to do-with His guidance."

The President took a deep breath and then continued. "George Washington has been attributed with saying that 'It is impossible to rightly govern the world without God and the Bible.' While the origin of this quote has been disputed by many, there is no question that our founding fathers believed this truth, although they would never force these noble convictions on anyone. Now, what I just said may have angered some of my constituents, but as a citizen of the United States, I am entitled to my own personal religious beliefs, just as each of you are. I have not been true to my own faith for many months; however, I will seek to administer my responsibilities from this day forward, according to the moral values that my faith calls me to do." President Duncan was uncertain about how this statement would be accepted, but his words reflected a man who had experienced a tremendous awakening.

Back at the Crawford residence, Scott and Russell sat, captivated by the President's speech. They wanted to talk, but restrained themselves so they wouldn't miss anything he was saying. This was by far, the most important address either of them had ever heard any President give to the nation.

In the White House, Ellen Duncan sat in a room near the Oval Office with Aaron Crosby, watching the speech by television, in amazement. Both had anguished for days, even weeks over many of the decisions the President had been making. *"This is the man I married 25 years ago,"* she thought to herself. Ellen had watched her husband struggling inwardly for weeks. She knew that it was a battle between what he knew was right, and what he felt he had to do for the sake of his political party. As she watched his speech progress, the first lady knew that he had finally overcome his struggle.

"And if I may," the President pressed on, "I would like to clarify this country's relationship with our greatest ally in the Middle East. For too long, we have wavered between our relationship with Israel and the desire to live peaceably with the entire world. But in such a large world, it's just not possible to hold everyone's hand. History will show that in all of our efforts to appease the numerous demands of the enemies of Israel, this has never resulted in peace, nor has it won their favor. And history will also demonstrate that we have never had a more faithful ally in the Middle East than Israel herself. Regarding my previous recommendations toward this great country, my actions were in serious error. We must no longer allow ourselves to waver in our support of our ally, but give her our full and unreserved backing. This may anger some within their region, but our prayers will continue to go out that they will find peace for themselves." While the multi-faced crisis in the Middle East could change regardless of how he moved, President Duncan was fully resolved to re-affirm the country's commitment to stand behind Israel.

"I understand that a bill is under debate in Congress right now that would halt all support of any country who is an avowed enemy of our sister state. But I'm going to take it a step further. Tomorrow, I will ask Congress to expedite this resolution, and to send me a bill that will end all U.S. support of any and all foreign nations that avow themselves as an enemy of the United States, or Israel, or any of our other allies, and who hold as their purpose to destroy our Judeo Christian Values.

I will also ask Congress to review national policy on hate crimes against religious groups. This country cannot continue to persecute or prosecute individuals simply for speaking and living by their religious convictions. This is a value that was brought to our shores by the original settlers, and we have a responsibility to protect this sacred trust."

The President took a breath before winding down his speech. "Realizing the role that a leader can play in the building up, or tearing down of a nation, and in light of the upcoming presidential elections just a few short months away, I ask you to join me in prayer that America will elect the right person, regardless of political party or affiliation. Over the past several years, America has slipped into a spiral toward destruction. But if what recently took place on Capitol Hill is representative of what can happen when man puts their hope in God, then I have no doubt this nation can undo all that has been torn down in our society. For the remainder of my term, I will endeavor to lead this great country as one nation under God.

In closing this evening, as Joshua, the mighty warrior leader of Israel once told the nation of Israel, '...if serving the

LORD seems undesirable to you, then choose for yourselves this day whom you will serve, whether the gods your ancestors served beyond the Euphrates, or the gods of the Amorites, in whose land you are living. But as for me and my household, we will serve the LORD.' [34] Thank you, and may God bless America."

The scene on the television once again switched back to the anchor desk where Marvin Maddox sat with his hands folded, reflecting on the amazing change that had come over the President. "Ladies and Gentlemen, what an astounding address we have just heard," he said with enthusiasm. "Tonight, the President spoke of a change that has swept over both Houses of Congress; but I believe this change may have reached all the way to the Oval Office. The President declared that such a change could only be the hand of God," the news anchor began to slow down to conclude his summary. "May God allow this refreshing transformation to sweep over our homes, schools and Churches throughout the entire nation. So that's it, for tonight. I'll see you back tomorrow evening at six thirty, Eastern Time."

14

Afterword-It's Time to Take a Stand

"May God arise, may his enemies be scattered; may his foes flee before him." -Psalm 68:1

You may have noticed that several sub-plots were not resolved in the preceding chapters; the national budget crisis, the Charleston bombing incident, same-sex marriage, a Supreme Court decision, and the presidential election. That's because I want you to ask, *"What happened?"* or better still, *"What could happen?"* The issues in this book are pounding at the door of America's, and of the Christian Church's leadership today. By the time this book is published the U.S. Supreme Court may have already ruled on a very significant case. Many fear that at least one of the rulings will uphold anti-biblical values. Such a ruling would inevitably increase attacks on our Christian freedoms. If that happens, this would not have to be a finality. We, as God's Church have surrendered to the secular mentality that the Supreme Court of the United States is the supreme law of the universe. We have decided that man's way is better than God's way; but in reality God's Word is the absolute end of all truth, regardless of what our modern culture claims that it is. Sadly, many professing Christians no longer accept the Holy Bible, as God's inspired Word. Equally as bad, these individuals do not

209

believe in *biblical inerrancy*. This belief states that the Bible contains errors; therefore it cannot be relied on as the ultimate end of all truth. When this is man's view of God, he has placed man's law over God's. This is idolatry; but when the Church reaches the point that we fear offending God more than we do offending man, we will begin to see a return to morality. It can start with you. It can start with me.

40 to 50 years ago, the Church played a large part in most American's lives. It was respected by people from all facets of society. Church members lived by higher standards than the non Church-going population. The main focus of Sunday morning Church worship service was to hear a message from the Lord, brought by God's servant, the pastor. The purpose of this weekly message was to change lives and challenge believers to live more like Jesus. Even though the country was experiencing a strong cultural upheaval during the hippie movement when drugs and "free love" were running rampant, people's hearts and minds were generally more spiritually centered. Over the years we have lost some of that identity, to the point that there are almost no standards for right living.

Many Churches today are nothing less than an entertainment center, with fog machines blowing smoke and other props used to generate more excitement for the worship hour; an inspirational talk with little spiritual substance will make the attenders feel better about themselves. In order to be "relevant" to modern culture, these fellowships are heavily concerned with keeping up with the latest fads and trends of the world. But the world looks on from the outside in disdain at a people-group that claims to be different, yet lives by their same mores.

To illustrate, several years ago I began visiting a bar in our small town. Being raised in a Christian home as a preacher's kid, I had never before set foot in a "joint" in my entire life. I was a little uncomfortable when I first walked in. In fact I parked on the back side of the parking lot so no one would see the preacher's truck sitting next to the town's bar, even though I knew the Lord was leading me to go there. I felt out of place. Perhaps that's how Jesus' disciples felt when he led them into the forbidden land, Samaria? [36]   I started going every week, and began looking forward to talking and shooting pool with a few of the regulars; and losing quite a few matches! I don't get to go as often as I once did, but a few lessons were learned during my many visits. The patrons of this particular bar were more regular than many professing Christians are to their own Churches; there was genuineness in the relationships. They didn't claim to be someone they were not. I also ran into one or two Church folks in the bar. They disappeared after learning that a local pastor was apt to pop in! Many of the patrons had a Christian upbringing or at least a strong Christian influence in their earlier lives. One of the non-Church going regulars told me he saw no difference in the lives of Christians and the way that he lived.

This demonstrates how some of the Church has lost its relevance by lowering its standards to the point that sinners see no reason to pass their time in a Christian worship service. If we were to show through our own lifestyles that the message of the Bible *does* change lives, we might see more souls being saved. Hold that thought. In short, how can we change the world, when there seems to be no difference between us and the world?

The present circumstances in America paint a gloomy picture of the future; terrorism is rampant, our prisons are overcrowded, and violence continues to spread around our country regardless of our efforts to pass laws to make us safer. Teen pregnancy is out of control, and 40% of adults no longer see the institution of marriage as even being relevant. [37] Our children are taught to exercise good judgment and use proper protection when engaging in sexual intercourse, rather than abstinence before marriage.

But the hot topic of today often doesn't involve these statistics. If I were to ask, *"What is the greatest danger facing America today?"* some of the answers are inevitable: ISIS, unemployment, or perhaps nuclear war; maybe same-sex marriage or abortion? These issues are indeed a threat to the stability of our society, but I propose that *the greatest danger to America is a Church that has turned its back on God and the authority of His Word, the Holy Bible*. After centuries of experiencing God's blessings, our materialistic culture has produced the greatest curse of all-a nation that no longer needs God.

Consider this: According to the 2014 General Social Survey, 7.5 million Americans have abandoned their religion since 2012. The study also found that 35 percent of people in the U.S. do not even attend church. [38] Gallup states that number to be much lower at 17.7%. [39] Another recent Gallup poll indicated that 77% of the adult population classify themselves as Christians. Additionally, 18% of Americans do not have an exact religious identity while 5% follow a non-Christian religion. [40] This leads one to wonder, "If the numbers are actually this high, what are the 77 percent doing to effect change in this godless society?" The Church has sung great hymns of faith through the centuries declaring its power:

At the sign of triumph Satan's host doth flee;

212

on then, Christian soldiers, on to victory!
Hell's foundations quiver at the shout of praise;
brothers, lift your voices, loud your anthems raise. [41]

Another more contemporary chorus issues this proclamation:

We've got the power in the name of Jesus;
We've got the power in the name of the LORD;
Though Satan rages, we cannot be defeated;
For we've got the power in the name of the LORD. [42]

So, where is this power that the Christian Church possesses? Instead of advancing as God's mighty army, much of the modern Church is merely marking time while waiting for Jesus to return. Or what's worse, retreating as threats come against it from every front. Like the proverbial frog in the kettle, we have become immune to the attacks against our values, standing idly by as our national leaders sneer at the Bible and threaten our Christian beliefs while ignoring the slaughter of hundreds of Christian believers in foreign countries. Many Christians have thrown up their hands in despair, lamenting with the rest of the world that "There is no hope," when in fact, we have the *only* hope; Jesus Christ. We too, are slipping into darkness, instead of turning the world "from darkness to light." [43]

In the movie, *"Sheffey, the Saint of the Wilderness,"* that tells about the life of the 19th century circuit-riding evangelist, at the film's climax, Robert Sheffey makes this statement:
"Every time we give up a part of our faith to fit into the ways of the world, we lose it forever. We lose a precious part of God's promise, sacrificed to the world, and the world will never give it

213

back. And some day, when the world tells us that we cannot have our religion, except where they say, and God is driven from our schools and our government, and our homes, then God's people can look back and know that our religion was not taken from us. It was given up, handed over, bit by bit, until there was nothing left." [44]

America has not yet reached that point, but we stand dangerously close to falling over a spiritual cliff that could completely destroy our Christian liberties as we know them today. But in spite of what modern doomsayers and the national media say about the decline and inevitable fall of our nation, nothing is so broken that it can't be fixed, if we seek God's hand of intervention. *"Surely the arm of the LORD is not too short to save, nor his ear too dull to hear. But your iniquities have separated you from your God; your sins have hidden his face from you, so that he will not hear."* [45.1] Isaac Watts said, *"...we have reason to fear that our iniquities, our coldness in religion, and the general carnality of our spirits have raised a wall of separation between God and us: and we may add, the pride and perverse humour of infidelity, degeneracy, and apostasy from the Christian faith which have of late years broken out amongst us, seem to have provoked the Spirit of Christ to absent Himself much from our nation."* [45.2] Herein lies the reason why we as God's children have lost our power. Just as positive results were brought about by Congressman Edwards' personal actions in this book, the outcome of real issues in our own lives will be influenced by *our* response, as God's Church. *I am convinced that two praying saints have more power to change America's course than the entire Legislative, Judicial and Executive branches of the US government combined.*

But how?

214

The great Old Testament prophet, Elijah may have asked himself this same question at some point in his life. God used him to call a backslidden nation back to right living. Elijah was called to stand up to Ahab, the seventh king of Israel. The nation of Israel had a chronic problem of following after the nations around them and falling into worship of their idols, in spite of God's command not to bow down to other gods or idols.[46]   The nation progressively drifted further from God, and when Ahab succeeded his father as king, the narrative of his legacy was that he *"did more evil in the eyes of the* LORD *than any of those before him."* [47]   During Elijah's first meeting with Ahab, he appeared with a strong message: *"As surely as there is a living God, it will not rain for the next several years, until I say that it will."* [48]

Baal was revered as the storm and fertility god, along with Asherah, his female counterpart. The people of that day believed it was Baal who sent rain to water the crops. Baal worship sometimes included perverted sexual activity and child sacrifices. This licentious worship was introduced to Israel after Ahab married the Phoenician princess, Jezebel, who brought along her pagan gods, rituals and worship.   The purpose of Elijah's ultimatum was to show Ahab and Israel how these idols were powerless to water their crops, produce a harvest or provide for any of their needs. After confronting Ahab, Elijah vanished, seemingly from the face of the earth. And there was no rain. The ground became parched to the point that even the rivers and streams dried up.

Some three years after the drought began, God sent Elijah to appear before Ahab, again. When he met the king, he immediately proposed a showdown to settle the issue once and for all. Elijah stood face to face with King Ahab, and told him to call all the people to Mount Carmel. As was common for customs of idol worship, this "high place" was a familiar location where Baal worship took place. It was no coincidence that Elijah called the people to this mountain. He intended to invade the Devil's territory. When they arrived, he asked them, *"How long are you going to straddle the fence? If the LORD is God, follow Him; but if Baal is God, then follow him."* [49]

Then he threw down the gauntlet and told them to build an altar for the sacrifice. The God who answered by fire would be God. So, a bull was slaughtered and laid on the altar of Baal. The prophets cried out to Baal while Elijah looked on quietly. But there was no fire. At noon, he began to taunt them, making them even more desperate. "Shout a little louder," he said. "He must have gotten distracted. Maybe he's too busy, or he may be on vacation. Or, perhaps he's taking a nap!"

The worshippers of Baal became even more determined, and shouted louder, even cutting themselves with their swords, trying to get Baal's attention. But it didn't happen. This went on until mid day. Finally that evening, Elijah called the crowd to gather around. They had prayed to Baal, but to no avail.

Now it was his turn, and the Bible tells us that Elijah "repaired the altar of the Lord, that had been torn down." [50] He dug a large trench around the altar, arranged the wood on it, and then laid the bull to sacrifice in pieces on the wood. Then he told them to pour twelve large containers of water on the altar and sacrifice. The water ran down the altar and filled the trench.

At the time of sacrifice, the prophet Elijah stepped forward and prayed: *"LORD, the God of Abraham, Isaac and Israel, let it be known today that You are God in Israel and that I am Your servant and have done all these things at Your command. Answer me, LORD, answer me, so these people will know that You, LORD, are God, and that You are turning their hearts back again."* [51]

Then a miracle happened.

Fire fell from heaven burning up the sacrifice and wood. The fire was so hot that it consumed even the stones and the soil, licking up the water in the trench. The results were equally phenomenal. These hardened people fell on their faces and cried out, *"The LORD-He is God! The LORD-He is God!"* [52]

And the Bible goes on to say that God sent rain on the land. But after this victory, Elijah was threatened by Jezebel, who had heard her prophets had been put to death. He was so afraid that he ran for his life. But throughout this ordeal, although he was reminded of how powerfully the Lord had used him, he became discouraged, even to the point that he wanted to die.

Think about it. At the showdown, there were 450 prophets of Baal, and 400 prophets of Asherah. Elijah stood outnumbered 850 to one. But God said, *"...I reserve seven thousand in Israel— all whose knees have not bowed down to Baal and whose mouths have not kissed him."* [53] An entire nation returned to God, because one man took a stand. You may be asking, "How can I bring about such a change as this? After all, he was a great prophet from the Bible!" Here's the answer. The Bible says that *"Elijah was a human being, even as we are. He prayed earnestly that it would not rain, and it did not rain on the land for three and a half years."* [54]

A Spiritual revival is not only possible; it is necessary if we will survive as a nation. Our future depends on our obedience, or disobedience to call out to God and repent of our

217

personal and national sins; and as Elijah, call this nation to return to the old standards of true Bible living. While the world will continue to become more evil in the days leading up to our Lord's soon return, [55] such a revival would produce pockets of peace around the nation, and conceivably the entire nation. And while men will continue to mock God and ridicule us for our Christian faith, [56] godly leaders, sympathetic to our rights as believers could enable many thousands of souls to be won into God's kingdom.

This kind of awakening is birthed by fervent, heart-felt prayer. Not just talking to God, but also *listening* to His voice. *Prayer is what shields, or protects us from any influence that hinders our relationship with Christ.* This is of particular importance, if not most important of all. Our personal prayer lives will check us spiritually, keep our thoughts under control, and remind us of areas that need changing in our own lives. Prayer will also give us a more powerful witness to the world around us. Our environments affect us as they do every human on earth. Current events in the public arena are a major influence on our lives today. So we are vulnerable to the issues that are so hostile to our core values. When our beliefs are challenged, we will respond in some manner, whether good or bad.

We are saturated by daily news from the time we turn the television on in the morning, or check our email when we arrive at work. Social media is another of the most visible platforms that communicates these events, and trends that affect us personally. This is an area that I personally had to learn to bring under control. I had found myself becoming more involved in my social media interaction, focusing on many of these matters in ways that can't bring about any positive change. So I made a conscious choice to back off from the online political jabbing, and as I read some of these comments that flood my page, focus my energy praying for America to return Christian men and women to our legislature. And I pray for the ungodly principles that threaten our Christian liberties to be overthrown.

Am I saying that Christians should not engage in the political arena? By no means! We *should* be verbal about our beliefs. Our voices *must* be heard. It's time for the Church to rise up in unified, righteous indignation against the world who is unified in its battle to hush the voice of Christianity in our society. But when engaging in conversations in any public forum, whether social media, or in person, not get taken in by the same spirit that possesses the world. If we fight the devil on his terms, we'll lose every time. We need to work to elect good godly men and women in our public places. If we don't, that position will be filled with someone who will fight to destroy our Christian values. But we must guard ourselves against the temptation of fighting the personalities, rather than the principles. Don't allow the controversy to control our time and thinking. The apostle, Paul said it this way. *"We demolish arguments and every pretension that sets itself up against the knowledge of God, and we take captive every thought to make it obedient to Christ."* 57

We also pray believing, because there is power in prayer. If this were not so, then prayer would be pointless. In fact, reading the Bible would be pointless except for literary enrichment, because it is full of instructions on how and why we should pray. James, the half brother of Jesus told his readers that, *"The prayer of a righteous person is powerful and effective."* 58 Jesus taught, and demonstrated the power of prayer, both in His public ministry and private life. It was His desire that His

219

followers would comprehend the prominence that prayer must hold in their daily lives and ministry, and He desires the same for us today. If you take a close look at the work of Jesus' disciples after He returned to heaven, you will see a close relationship between their prayer life and the power that was demonstrated in the early Church. These were truths that those we refer to as the "old timers," or previous generations in our Churches, had a firm understanding of. They prayed passionately on a daily basis. Churches across America had a mid-week "prayer meeting," which was a gathering in which the focus of the hour was to *pray*. We should take back this same urgency in our Churches today. Let us not be so attached to the latest trends (many that will vanish within 10 years) that we forsake Jesus' own assessment of the Lord's house; that it should be "a house of prayer." [59]

During the times in our country's history when prayer was the focus of the Church, there were more souls being saved. The crime rates were down, and even though people still lived immoral lives, it was less rampant; out of wedlock births were not the norms of society.

One such movement, birthed by a strong emphasis on corporate prayer came to be known as the Third Great Awakening of America in the mid-19th century. In 1857 America was living in a time of prosperity, with a strong economy. As is often the case when things are going right, there was a widespread indifference toward God, and spiritual concerns.

But a 48 year old businessman named Jeremiah Lamphier, of New York City felt a burden to simply pray. He rented a room where he invited the community to pray each Wednesday between twelve noon and one o'clock in the afternoon. The first meeting was held on September 23rd, with only a few attending. Two days later the Bank of Pennsylvania in Philadelphia folded, shocking the entire nation. The next week, 20 people arrived for the prayer hour. Then, on October 10, the New York stock market crashed, causing the loss of numerous jobs, and closing down businesses around the nation. The national sentiment of prosperity and self sufficiency was replaced with uncertainty and widespread panic, as hundreds filed bankruptcy and began adjusting to a lifestyle of poverty. Within six months the small crowd of less than ten grew to a throng of 10,000 people and above, calling out to God in prayer all over New York. The weekly prayer gatherings quickly moved to daily meetings.

This spiritual awakening wasn't confined to one city, but spread around the nation, with thousands gathering each day in the various cities, spurring several notable ministries, such as the Moody Bible Institute, in Chicago. Churches were filled to capacity for months. It has been estimated that one million souls in America alone were converted to Christianity in less than two years, with a population of only 30 million. This time of spiritual awakening wasn't marked with any outward manifestations, as had occurred in previous spiritual revivals, but a simple compulsion to pray. The great revivalist, Charles Finney commented, *"The general impression seemed to be, 'We have had instruction until we are hardened; it is now time for us to pray.' "* [60]

If we desire to see such an awakening today, it must start on this playing field. It's time to lay down worldly devices, and pick up the greatest weapon against the enemy we have at our disposal. We should pray about everything that affects our lives, whether personal, professional or public concerns; family, friends, associates, and even government. Pray for your pastor, that he or she will boldly preach God's uncompromised Word under anointing from the Holy Spirit. Pastors are facing increasing pressure to "back off" of certain themes found in the Bible. If we succumb to pressure to leave one topic out of our preaching, the world will pressure us to compromise one step further. Why? It is the preaching of God's Word that leads to Holy Spirit conviction of sin.

Imagine what would happen if we re-established the "family altar," or family devotional time in our homes. Single mothers who are fighting the unimaginable social issues that come from the lack of a father figure would see a change in their family lives; in fact the divorce rate would plummet, and the nuclear family would once again become the foundation of a sound society.

Picture the outcome if Christians began praying for our public officials in our Church services, in small groups, and even in our homes. The nation would no longer tolerate legislations whose avowed purposes are to eradicate Christianity from our society. Our government could experience a revival within its own ranks, and operate on a completely different plane than its current practices. National legislation would reflect good morals, not because they would be forcing Christianity on the world, but because Christians would begin to put good moral people in office. The federal deficit would be wiped out, and the nation would experience the prosperity it once enjoyed. America would have a greater witness, and once again command the world-influence it once held.

As previously mentioned, the Supreme Court will be ruling at any time on at least one critical issue that could destroy our Christian heritage and change our country forever. In the human realm, it may seem hopeless. But in the spiritual realm, God can change circumstances when there is no human way to control it. Our prayers could hasten it.

Contrary to the belief of advocates for a secular society, our founding fathers recognized the importance of a national dependency on God, and godly morals. The Second Continental Congress met on June 12, 1775, shortly after the war for American independence began. Recognizing the seriousness of this conflict that could destroy the thirteen colonies, they called for a national day of "public humiliation, fasting and prayer." The language of this historic document reflects the Christian faith that the members of this Congress held to, and dependence on the God of Christianity and none other, to protect and sustain them.[61]

While these men never sought to restrict any one's freedom to worship, whatever their religious belief, they never endorsed a deity outside of the God of the Holy Bible. And even though the framers of our Constitution never intended to have a single State-sponsored religion, there is an abundance of historical evidence that demonstrates that these founding fathers fully intended for America to be governed by good moral principles. Since the present philosophy of a separation between Church and State is a stronghold chained by spiritual forces, [62] today it would be difficult to pass any legislation that would encourage living according to our Judeo Christian values. Our only hope therefore, is call out to God to restore our land to right living.

Our prayer must then be followed by petitioning our government leaders. Not only is this one of the constitutional freedoms that we enjoy today, but also a biblical practice.

The Bible contains a very unique story in the Old Testament Book of Esther. Although it has no mention of God, this book shows the providence of God and His hand of protection upon His people. The Jews had returned from their exile from the Babylonian captivity around 536 B.C. after Persia conquered Babylon. But some chose to remain in the foreign land, even though they had been encouraged by the prophets to go back home once they were freed.

Several years passed, and King Xerxes had Queen Vashti removed from her place of honor because she had openly disrespected him. Xerxes commissioned a widespread search for a new queen that lasted for months. A beautiful woman named Esther was ultimately chosen to replace Vashti. Esther was a Jew, whose family had remained in the land. After her parents died, her cousin, Mordecai adopted her as his own daughter. Mordecai asked Esther not to reveal that she was a Jew before she entered her new life as queen.

Over the course of time, Mordecai refused to bow down to one of the king's highest officials named Haman; his Jewish faith demanded that he bow before no one but the LORD his God. But Haman, full of conceit, was angered to the point that he plotted not only to harm Mordecai, but all of his people within the land. Haman led Xerxes to believe that the Jews were living in rebellion to his law, and manipulated the king to have all of the Jews annihilated. Unbeknown to the king that he was being trapped, he issued an order for the Jew's destruction; men and women, the elderly and children alike. When this news was announced throughout the land, Mordecai, along with all the Jews was distressed, and sent a message to Queen Esther, requesting her to intercede for the Jews to the king.

The new queen was initially reluctant to present the petition to the king. The law did not allow anyone to enter the king's presence uninvited. She would run the risk of death by entering his chamber unless he extended his scepter in peace toward her. But she sent word for the people to fast with her for three days, and then she would go. Esther took the issue to Xerxes, regardless of its consequences to her. After she approached the king, he granted her request to spare the Jews. When King Xerxes learned that Haman had plotted this scheme, he was hung on a gallows that he had prepared for Mordecai to be executed on. [63]

The root of the conflict between Haman and Mordecai was spiritual, just as are the increasing anti-Christian sentiments in America today. Our Constitution guarantees citizens the right to petition our government; and there is no such danger as Esther faced, to anyone who chooses to exercise this freedom of petition in America. However, we as Christians face increasing ridicule, and hostile opposition from those who hate Christianity, and who we stand for. We too, must stand with our brothers and sisters when they are wrongfully persecuted, even if it were to cost us our freedom, or lives.

So, how can we petition our government? This should begin at the local level by meeting, and building relationships with your town or city councilmen, and mayor. Develop a dialogue with them to express your concerns that America, and even the towns and cities should be governed by Christian morals. Assure them of your prayers for God to use them as His instruments of peace. Just as it is our responsibility to elect national leaders to stand for godly principles, we must also elect local officials who will do the same.

As the occasion arises, contact your state and national congressmen to demonstrate your concerns, and prayerful support that he or she will make the right decisions. Attend local "townhouse meetings" when you learn a congressman will be in town. When you are unable to attend, you can communicate effectively via telephone and email. Thirty years ago, it took more effort to contact your state senator or congressman, but today we can reach them with the touch of a button at our fingertips. Don't be afraid to develop an active dialogue with your elected leaders through their local offices. Encourage your friends and associates to become active in expressing their ideas and concerns to their representatives.

And, perhaps the greatest form of petition is by going to the booth. Good men and women have been put out of office, or never made it to public service because God's people failed to lend their support and vote. It's easy to engage in debate over who the best candidate is, or why one candidate is unfit for office; but this isn't the platform that counts. Americans demonstrate power by going to the polls and casting our vote. This is a sacred freedom we must never forsake. And for those who may have, it must be taken back. Your vote could change the entire path our country is traveling today. Remember, *"All that is necessary for evil to succeed is that good men do nothing."* [64]

Jesus taught his followers to be "the salt of the earth." He also gave a sobering reminder of what happens when salt loses its taste: *"It is no longer good for anything, except to be thrown out and trampled underfoot."* [65]   This is what God sees when he looks on a lukewarm Church that has bowed to the humanistic philosophies of our society. So His will for the Church is to change our world. Remember that we have the right, and responsibility, as believers to put men and women in office who stand for the living Word of God. God will hold His people accountable for putting officials in places of authority who oppose His right standards for living. If we want to see America restored to its former glory, we must return the land to her true moral values.

I call for Christians to rise up against every principle and philosophy that violates biblical standards for living. This is a call to *repentance*. A universal spiritual revival can only begin on our knees. The theme of repentance was the very first record of Jesus' teaching, found in Matthew's Gospel. There is a gap with nothing said of Him between the age of twelve and about thirty, with no narrative about His specific life events during this time. But when Jesus re-emerged on the scene, He first spent forty days and forty nights fasting and praying in the wilderness, and then being tempted by the devil. After this preparation for His public ministry, the Bible tells us that, *"From that time on Jesus began to preach, 'Repent, for the kingdom of heaven has come near.'"*[66]

The word, *repent*, in the Greek μετάνοια (*Metanoia*) is translated as, "a changing of the mind." [67] It is found some 24 times in the New Testament. This signifies a willful decision relating to one's personal actions. Christians are expected to walk above the physical plane that nonbelievers live by. When we stumble and "fall," meaning, when we sin, we turn and walk away from it, instead of allowing it to continue in our lives.

Many years ago when I was in the ROTC, one of our regular activities was a weekly drill, marching through a series of routine commands; "A-ten-hut!" (attention!), right and left flanks, and "about face," which is the simple command to turn around and march in the opposite direction. When marching in a platoon or company, if one person didn't follow a command, their inaction, or wrong action affected the entire platoon. Imagine this. You're marching, in unison with a platoon of 50 soldiers or seamen. When the platoon leader gives the command,

"About Face," the entire company turns around, but you continue to march straight ahead, ever so focused. Within seconds you collide with the person in front of you. Both of you are thrown off balance, causing a collision with another soldier, and another. Rifles are smashing together. The platoon comes to a grinding halt, and must be called back to proper formation before resuming the march. If you are somehow able to catch yourself and jump back into formation with the others as soon as you miss the command, the company may be slowed down momentarily, but you can continue to march.

If we allow sin into our personal lives, it causes a breakdown of our relationship with God, as well as the structure within the body of Christian believers. The Church loses its effectiveness. While many people try to justify wrongdoing by the excuse, "I'm hurting no one but myself," our actions do affect everyone around us. Today, many within the Church ranks are not marching completely in step with our Savior's commands. It's time to stop and consider what has happened by allowing sin to corrupt the body of believers. Then we must repent, or turn in the opposite direction, and live in obedience to our instructions, found in the Bible. When we reach this point, the Church will once again live and walk in the power that God has entrusted to us.

Secondly, I call my readers to *restoration.* Remember Elijah, who rebuilt the altar of the Lord that had been torn down? The altar in the Bible was a place of sacrifice. The blood of an innocent animal had to be shed in order to cover the peoples' sins, thereby restoring their relationship with God. But when Jesus shed his blood on the cross, he became the eternal sacrifice that took away the sins of the entire world. It is no longer necessary to offer a blood sacrifice at the temple, because He paid the eternal price.   It's time to rebuild the altar of the Lord in the Church today; not an altar for blood sacrifice, but an altar of *personal* sacrifice in our daily lives. Paul explained this in his epistle to the Romans:

"With eyes wide open to the mercies of God, I beg you, my brothers, as an act of intelligent worship, to give him your bodies, as a living sacrifice, consecrated to him and acceptable by him. Don't let the world around you squeeze you into its own mould, but let God re-mould your minds from within, so that you may prove in practice that the plan of God for you is good, meets all his demands and moves towards the goal of true maturity." [68]

    In contrast to Old Testament sacrifices, this is a *living* sacrifice.[69]   Since our body is the temple of the Holy Spirit,[70] we should no longer live like the world; instead, we must surrender the pleasures that hinder our relationship with Him. This doesn't mean that we can't live happy lives. Rather, that we must be willing to lay down anything that is in opposition to God's Word; even when everyone around us is "doing it." When we follow these biblical standards of conduct, the world will see Jesus living in us. *Then* we can be the change agents that we were called to be.

    And finally, I call for a modern-day *reformation*. Yes, I'm speaking of a radical movement. It's time to take a stand. But I'm not talking about another sit-in, or parade, or wear a ribbon campaign to bring awareness to some social injustice. These events can have a useful purpose, if focused in the right direction. But the Christian community doesn't need a million man march on the Washington Mall to get the world's attention. We don't need a protest with signs outside the Supreme Court to sway the opinions of the nine justices, either. What the Church needs-what the world needs, is something that will get *God's* attention.

To do this, those of us who are Christians should simply *live* like Christians. Having committed ourselves to Christ, as our Lord and Savior, let as commit ourselves to a local Church congregation, and attend regularly-not to merely be seen by others around us, or to fulfill our sacred duty. We go to Church, to allow God's Word to challenge and change our lives. To simply reiterate the message stated above, we must once again call our Churches to corporate and consistent prayer. Not on occasion, or after a disaster hits the country, but a regularly weekly (and daily) time when we call out to God for His mercy, His guidance in our lives, and the lives of our leaders; for the salvation of our family, friends-and foes, and for Divine protection. Let us find a place of daily, personal solitude with the Lord, seeking His presence in our land. He promises to hear our prayer when we cry out to Him. It's time to take a stand.

And in our Church services, we must pray for revival. Our hearts must scream for spiritual renewal. While we can't bring our own revival, men and women do play a part in allowing it to happen in our lives. In fact, God's Word demands that we do our part (2 Chronicles 7:14). This promise for spiritual renewal and national healing is conditional, based on our obedience to His Word. As we obey, we will create conditions that are conducive to receiving this promise. God is faithful!

Should the Lord continue to wait, yet longer to return for His Church, we will face harder battles than we struggle with today. Let us depend on His Word, and His power to fight these battles for us.

230

^{10} Finally, be strong in the Lord and in His mighty power. ^{11} Put on the full armor of God, so that you can take your stand against the devil's schemes. ^{12} For our struggle is not against flesh and blood, but against the rulers, against the authorities, against the powers of this dark world and against the spiritual forces of evil in the heavenly realms. ^{13} Therefore put on the full armor of God, so that when the day of evil comes, you may be able to stand your ground, and after you have done everything, to stand. ^{14} Stand firm then, with the belt of truth buckled around your waist, with the breastplate of righteousness in place, ^{15} and with your feet fitted with the readiness that comes from the gospel of peace. ^{16} In addition to all this, take up the shield of faith, with which you can extinguish all the flaming arrows of the evil one. ^{17} Take the helmet of salvation and the sword of the Spirit, which is the word of God. Ephesians 6:10-17

Bibliography

1. *A Teacher's Guide to Religion in the Public Schools.* Nashville, TN: First Amendment Center, 1999. Print.

2. *An Overview of Relations between Israel and Palestine.* University of Colorado Law Library, n.d. Web. 22 Apr. 2015.

3. Arberry, A. J. *The Koran Interpreted.* London: Allen & Unwin, 1955. Print.

4. Barton, David. "Church in the U.S. Capitol." *Wall Builders.* N.p., 10 Nov. 2005. Web. 22 April, 2015.

5. "Can Private Schools Discriminate Against Students?" *Lawyers.com Your Legal Solution Stops Here.* n.p., n.d. Web. 22 Apr. 2015.

6. Collins, Gary R., Ph.D. *Christian Counseling, A Comprehensive Guide.* 3rd ed. Thomas Nelson, 2007. Print.

7. Colson, Charles W., and Ellen Santilli. Vaughn. *Against the Night: Living in the New Dark Ages.* Ann Arbor, MI: Vine, 1989. Print.

8. Edman, V. Raymond. *Finney on Revival: A Study of Charles Finney's Revival Methods and Message.* n.p.: Bethany House, 2000. Print.

9. "Focus on the Family Position Statement on Same-Sex 'Marriage' and Civil Unions" *CitizenLink.com - A Public Policy Partner of Focus on the Family.* Focus On The Family, n.d. Web. 21 Apr. 2015.

10. Gates, Gary J., and Frank Newport. "Gallup Special Report: New Estimates of the LGBT Population in the United States - See More At: Http://williamsinstitute.law.ucla.edu/research/census-lgbt-demographics-studies/gallup-lgbt-pop-feb-2013/#sthash.vwKMC2tf.dpuf." *The Williams Institute*. The Williams Institute, Feb. 2013. Web. 22 Apr. 2015.

11. Ghattas, R. G., and Carol Ghattas. *A Christian Guide to the Qur'an: Building Bridges in Muslim Evangelism*. Grand Rapids, MI: Kregel Publications, 2009. Print.

12. Graham, Billy. "Billy Graham: 'My Heart Aches for America'." *Billy Graham Evangelistic Association*. Billy Graham Evangelistic Association, 19 July 2012. Web. 17 Apr. 2015.

13. Hananoki, Eric. "Fox News Contributor: Fifty Shades Of Grey And Gay Marriage Are Signs Of The Apocalypse." *Media Matters for America*. Media Matters for America, 11 Feb. 2015. Web. 17 Apr. 2015.

14. Hopper, Jessica. "Marriage Obsolete?" *ABC World News*. ABC News, 18 Nov. 2010. Web. 22 Apr. 2015.

15. "Israel Under Fire." *Israel Defense Forces*. Israel Defense Forces, n.d. Web. 22 Apr. 2015.

16. "Jefferson's Letter to the Danbury Baptists." *The Heritage Foundation*. The Heritage Foundation, n.d. Web. 22 April, 2015.

17. Lehman, Reid. *Discrimination in Hiring by Religious Organizations*. Miracle Hill Ministries, Greenville, SC. Leadership Development Seminar, 2001. Print.

18. "Matthew Shepard and James Byrd, Jr., Hate Crimes Prevention Act of 2009." *The United States Department of Justice*. The United States Department of Justice, n.d. Web. 22 Apr. 2015.

19. "Mayflower Compact." *All About History*. n.p., n.d. Web. 22 Apr. 2015.

20. Newport, Frank. "In U.S., 77% Identify as Christian." *Gallup*. Gallup, Inc., n.d. Web. 22 Apr. 2015.

21. Okbi, Yasser, and Maariv Hashavua. "Iranian Military Chief Threatens to 'wipe Tel Aviv off the Map'" *The Jerusalem Post*. The Jerusalem Post, 26 Feb. 2015. Web. 22 Apr. 2015.

22. Parsley, Rod. *Silent No More*. Lake Mary, FL: Charisma House, 2005. Print.

23. Phillips, J.B. *The New Testament in Modern English*. Harper Collins, 1962.

24. Rogers, Tim. *Sheffey*. Feature Film. Unusual Films, 1977. Produced by Bob Jones University, Greenville, SC. Distributed by Showforth Videos, Bob Jones University. DVD.

25. Safa, Reza F. *Inside Islam: Exposing and Reaching the World of Islam*. Orlando, FL: Creation House, 1996. Print.

26. Sage, Henry J. "The Second Continental Congress, 1775-1781." Henry J. Sage, 17 July 2013. Web. 22 Apr. 2015.

27. Shattuck, Kelly. "7 Startling Facts: An Up Close Look at Church Attendance in America." *Church Leaders*. Church Leaders, n.d. Web. 22 Apr. 2015.

28. Somashekhar, Sandhya. "Health Survey Gives Government Its First Large Scale Data on Gay, Bi-sexual Population." *The Washington Post-Health and Science*. The Washington Post, 15 July 2014. Web. 22 Apr. 2015.

29. Stott, John R. W. *Same-sex Partnerships?: A Christian Perspective*. Grand Rapids, MI: F.H. Revell, Reprint, 2000. Print.

30. "Student Bill of Rights." *Student Bill of Rights-FAQ*. Liberty Institute, n.d. Web. 22 April, 2015.

31. "Survey: Millions of Americans Have Abandoned Religion in Last 2 Years." *Relevant*. Relevant Magazine, 16 Mar. 2015. Web. 22 Apr. 2015.

32. "Teaching about Religion in Public Schools: Where Do We Go From Here?" The First Amendment Center/The Pew Forum, 20-22 May 2003. Web. 22 April, 2015.

33. *The Holy Bible, New International Version.* Colorado Springs, CO: Biblica, Inc., Copyright 2011. Used by permission. Print.

34. "The Time for Prayer: The Third Great Awakening." *Christianity Today Library*. Christianity Today, 1989. Web. 22 Apr. 2015.

35. Theriot, Kevin, Karen S. Prior, and Kristen Blair. "Three Views: Do the Common Core Education Standards Endanger Religious Freedom?" *Christianity Today*. Christianity Today, 22 Oct. 2014. Web. 22 Apr. 2015.

36. Vine, W. E. *Vine's Expository Dictionary of New Testament Words: Complete and Unabridged*. Westwood, NJ: Barbour, 1985. Print.

37. Walvoord, John F. and Roy B. Zuck. *The Bible Knowledge Commentary*. New Testament Edition. Colorado Springs, CO: Cook Communications Ministries, 2000. Print.

38. Watts, Isaac. "A Narrative of Surprising Conversions." Preface. *Jonathon Edwards on Revival*. Carlisle, PA: Banner of Truth Trust, 1994. 2-3. Print. First published in 1936.

39. "What Are the Five Pillars of Islam?" *A Brief Illustrated Guide to Understanding Islam*. n.p., n.d. Web. 22 April, 2015.

Notes/Works Cited

Preface
1. Colson, p. 10-11
2. Matthew 5:13
3. Galatians 1:8.9
4. 2 Chronicles 7:14
5. Psalm 85:6
6. Hananoki, Article
7. Graham, Billy, Article

Chapter 1
8. Exodus 32: 19
9. 2 Corinthians 7:13-14
10. 1 Kings 19:18

Chapter 3
11. A Brief Illustrated Guide, p. 1
12. The Ten Commandments were given to Moses from God on Mount Sinai. They are initially listed in Exodus 20, and then re-stated in Deuteronomy 5, in the Old Testament.

Chapter 4
13. Jeremiah 1:4-8
14. Wall Builders, p. 1.
15. Jefferson's letter, p. 1.   Note: While Jefferson expressed his utmost respect for a "wall of separation between Church and State," this in no way supports the modern doctrine that religion must be excluded from the public arena. After all, he concludes this same letter (in his office as President) with a prayer.
16. Romans 8:31

Chapter 6
17. Student Bill of Rights, Question 17
18. Three Views, p. 1.   Common Core may not directly address the issue of religious instruction, but trends in government intrusion on public education may open the door to wrongfully introduce religious instruction in public schools.
19. Teaching about Religion in Public Schools, p. 4.
20. Mayflower Compact, p. 1

Chapter 7
21. Matthew Shepard, p. 1

Chapter 8
22. Can Private Schools Discriminate, p. 1
23. Somashekhar, p. 1, Gates, p. 1
24. Mark 3:24
25. The Torah is the first five books of the Tanakh, the canon of the Hebrew Bible, and the Old Testament books of the Law; Genesis, Exodus, Leviticus, Numbers and Deuteronomy.
26. Genesis 15:18, 28:13
27. An Overview of Relations, p. 1
28. Israel Under Fire, p. 1-2.   In 2005, amid the protests of Jewish residents of Gaza, some 8,500 residents were removed from the Gaza Strip as a good-will gesture by Israel to reduce friction between Israel and the Palestinians; regardless of this extreme sacrifice, the violence toward Israel continued. Since

withdrawing, terrorists have fired more than 11,000 rockets directly into the small country.
29. Okbi, Yasser, p. 1.   Numerous such statements have been made in previous years, by Iranian President Mahmoud Ahmadinejad; in 2005, and even further back.

Chapter 9
30. Matthew 18:6

Chapter 12
31. I Samuel 18:5, 14-15, 30
32. Lehman, Discrimination in Hiring...
33. Acts 16:16-32
34. Luke 9:28-36

Chapter 13
35. Joshua 24:15

Chapter 14
36. John 4:1-38
37. Hopper, p. 1
38. Survey: Millions of Americans, p. 1
39. Shattuck, p. 1
40. Newport, p. 1
41. *Onward Christian Soldiers.*   Lyrics, Sabine Baring-Gould 1865, Music, Sir Arthur S. Sullivan, 1871
42. *We've Got The Power*, Words and music, LaVerne Tripp, Laverne Trip Ministries, Gallatin, TN. Copyright date unknown.
43. Acts 26:15-18
44. Rogers, DVD, Final Act
45. Isaiah 59:1-2
46. Exodus 20:3, Deuteronomy 5:7
47. 1 Kings 16:30
48. 1 Kings 17:1 Paraphrase
49. 1 Kings 18:21 Paraphrase
50. I Kings 18:30b.

51. 1 Kings 18:36-37
52. 1 Kings 18:39
53. 1 Kings 19:18 Note: The complete account of Elijah's challenge to Ahab is found in 1 Kings 18-19.
54. James 5:17
55. 2 Timothy 3:13
56. 2 Peter 3:3
57. 2 Corinthians 10:5
58. James 5:16
59. Matthew 21:13, see also Isaiah 56:7
60. The Time for Prayer, p. 1
61. Sage, p. 1
62. Ephesians 6:12
63. The entirety of this drama can be read in the Old Testament book of Esther.
64. http://www.searchquotes.com/search/Evil_Prevails_When_Good_Men_Do_Nothing/
    There are several variations of this quote...the most common by Philosopher, Edmund Burke
65. Matthew 5:13
66. Matthew 4:17
67. Vine, pp. 279-281
68. Romans 12:1-2, Phillips
69. Walvoord, p. 487
70. 1 Corinthians 6:19-20

Current Events

CE-1. The following reference is not an IRS issue, but an example of real life government
intrusion into Christian freedoms in America.http://www.rightwingwatch.org/content/barber-gay-marriage-will-be-sledgehammer-used-crush-church

CE-2 In December, 2014, an attorney for a Wisconsin group representing agnostics and atheists sent a letter to the small town of Jay, FL, claiming that a nativity display on public property is illegal. The town removed the display. It was acquired by a local Ministerial Association and placed near the town's main stoplight. http://www.northescambia.com/2014/12/nativity-scene-removed-from-jay-town-hall-after-lawyer-claims-its-illegal
Over the past several decades, challenges against the public display of religious symbols have increased dramatically. The following is an extensive informational letter from the *American Center for Law and Justice* on the legalities of public Christmas displays: http://defendchristmas.com/christmas-reality/legalities-of-public-christmas-displays/

CE-3 This paragraph does not reflect actual statistics, but shows what could eventually occur. As of the writing of this book, 37 States have legalized same-sex "marriage," with 13 still holding bans on the unbiblical unions. Several States' bans are currently being challenged in the courts, and the U.S. Supreme Court heard oral arguments for and against redefining marriage in America. The ruling on this case is expected to be handed down in June of 2015. http://gaymarriage.procon.org/view.resource.php?resourceID=004857

CE-4 Schools across the country have been introducing various forms of religious instruction, increasingly over the past several years while omitting equal, or any time to the tenets of   Christianity. http://www.washingtontimes.com/news/2013/nov/5/parents-slam-pro-islam-slant-florida-textbook/ http://insider.foxnews.com/2014/10/29/marine-dad-banned-school-after-complaining-about-islam-assignment

CE-5 In October of 2014, Annise Parker, the mayor of Houston, Texas subpoenaed the sermons of several pastors who openly opposed an equal rights ordinance for residents of the LGBTQ community. The city officials were attempting to see if these pastors' teaching may have encouraged efforts to have this law repealed. http://time.com/3514166/houston-pastors-sermons-subpoenaed/

CE-6 October 18, 2014 Donald and Evelyn Knapp, two Christian ministers who own a wedding chapel in Idaho, were told to perform same-sex weddings or face jail time. The chapel is registered as a "religious corporation" limited to performing "one-man-one-woman marriages as defined by the Holy Bible." http://radio.foxnews.com/toddstarnes/top-stories/city-threatens-to-arrest-ministers-who-refuse-to-perform-same-sex-weddings.html

CE-7 This is an actual proposal by Senator Rand Paul, cosponsor of S. 1316 the One Cent Solution/"Penny Plan." http://www.onecentsolution.org/2011/07/27/senator-rand-paul-and-sean-hannity-on-one-cent-solution/

CE-8 Former Arkansas Governor Mike Huckabee made the first part of this statement on the FOX Channel's *The Huckabee Show*, on Saturday, October 25, 2014.

CE-9 The enclosed link references how the distribution of religious literature has become a topic of heightened debate

over the years. While equal access statutes mandate that no religious literature may be disseminated to the exclusion of others, this has opened the door for some anti-Christian movements to get their foot in the door to provide material that is hostile to our Judeo-Christian values.
http://tampa.cbslocal.com/2014/09/16/satanic-temple-distributes-coloring-activity-books-in-florida-schools/

www.ingramcontent.com/pod-product-compliance
Lightning Source LLC
Chambersburg PA
CBHW060919040426
42445CB00011B/693